CRAFT SPIRIT WORLD

CRAFT SPIRIT WORLD

A guide to the artisan
spirit-makers and distillers
you need to try

EMILY MILES

Published in 2015 by Dog 'n' Bone Books
An imprint of Ryland Peters & Small Ltd

20–21 Jockey's Fields   341 E 116th St
London WC1R 4BW   New York, NY 10029

www.rylandpeters.com

10 9 8 7 6 5 4 3 2 1

A CIP catalog record for this book is available from the
Library of Congress and the British Library.

ISBN: 978 1 909313 53 8

Printed in China

Editor: Caroline West
Designer: Mark Latter
Photography credits: See page 160
Illustrator: Blair Frame

Commissioning editor: Pete Jorgensen
Art director: Sally Powell
Production controller: Sarah Kulasek-Boyd
Publishing manager: Penny Craig
Publisher: Cindy Richards

CONTENTS

Part 1

INTRODUCTION

You could be forgiven for thinking that skinny jeans, statement tattoos, and a luxuriant beard are mandatory for any aspiring craft distiller. And, while it is certainly true that a new generation of trend-focused, artisan obsessives are behind the emergence of boutique gins, vodkas, whiskies, and so on, the truth of the matter is: there is nothing new about small-batch distilling.

Whether in the drizzle-shrouded Highlands of Scotland, the sun-soaked villages of southern France, or the outbuildings of an American corn farm, bothy stills, portable pot stills, and moonshine rigs have been in operation for centuries, fulfilling that basic human need to take some organic matter and make it as alcoholic as possible.

In times past, these operations were, by their very nature, small-scale and, more often than not, illegal. Today, there is an energetic re-emergence of diminutive, boutique producers, a movement that started in America and is now spreading across the globe. This time, the aim isn't to dodge the tax man, but rather to keep things small and to keep them craft.

CRAFT BEER:
A BRIEF BUT RELEVANT DIGRESSION

Unless you have been on a 10-year detox, you're unlikely to have missed out on the stratospheric rise of the craft beer brewing industry. This global phenomenon—which has brought a multitude of interesting and innovative beers to market—started out in the United States. Previously renowned for having possibly the world's most insipid beer, a wave of small-scale producers set out to do things differently: these guys went back to the archives and re-introduced heritage hop varieties, sourced unusual grains, refocused on quality rather than quantity, and, it has to be said, did a pretty stellar job on the marketing front, too.

WHY IT MATTERS

The micro-brewers' provenance- and flavor-focused products hit just the spot with a surprisingly thirsty and receptive audience, and, as momentum grew, an increasing number of brewers hitched their fortunes to the craft bandwagon. And who could blame them? In 2013, one of the founding fathers of this beer renaissance, Jim Koch of the Boston Beer Company, became—according to Bloomberg Billionaires Index—the first craft brewing billionaire.

Over a decade or so, craft beer's growing impact established a new market of cognoscenti: consumers who were willing to go the extra mile—and fork out the extra dollars—for a product with provenance. Following on their heels came the Millennials—a generation weaned on the importance of choosing local produce and also seeking out authenticity and quality in what they consumed. After all, who wants to Instagram themselves drinking an identikit product? Beer, then, had laid the groundwork for a like-minded revolution in spirits. By the mid-Noughties, the time was ripe for an antidote to soulless, commercial column stills with their vast output and over-reliance on the marketing machine. What was needed was the craft distiller.

With authenticity, character, and creativity as their watchwords, the emergence of the craft and artisan spirit movement has been nothing short of thrilling. Producers are resuscitating old styles of liquor and inventing new ones, re-invigorating economies, inspiring and educating consumers, and—at the cocktail-making coalface—giving bartenders an exciting new stash of ingredients for their creations.

But what exactly is craft distilling? And where is it happening? To witness a microcosm of this spirited revolution in action, you need go no further than Distillery Row, Portland, Oregon.

DISTILLERY ROW

The profusion of Japanese selvedge denim, single-origin coffee, and packed bike racks gives you all the style clues you need about this area's ascendency. The unapologetically industrial quarter in Portland's south-east side, with boutique shops and eateries springing up in the old warehouse buildings, is at the heart of the craft distilling movement, not just in Oregon, but in the USA—and possibly even the world. The cluster of new artisan enterprises, hunkered together within a few miles of cheap real-estate, produces more than 20 different hard liquors—small-batch, hand-crafted, artisan stuff—that are all grouped together under the Distillery Row banner.

Eastside Distilling

Landing on the row in 2009, Eastside Distilling—which was founded by two friends Bill Adams and Lenny Gotter—initially started out as a rum distiller, before adding its award-winning bourbon and potato-based vodka to the collection. A big fan of the "holiday spirit," Yuletide sees seasonal specials, such as eggnog liqueur, on offer.

Craft spirits: Below Deck Coffee Rum; Below Deck Ginger Rum; Below Deck Silver Rum; Portland Potato Vodka; Burnside Bourbon; Cherry Bomb Whiskey; Oregon Marionberry Whiskey
Address: 1512 SE 7th Avenue, Portland, OR 97214
Web: eastsidedistilling.com

House Spirits

Founded in 2004 by Tom Mooney, House Spirits was at the grass roots of the craft revolution (see interview with Tom, on page 13). Initially taken to market in Bordeaux wine bottles, and distilled in a still which now sits in Portland Airport, Aviation American Gin was the spirit that made the company's name. Where other distillers on the Row have come and gone, House Spirits continues to endure.

Craft spirits: Aviation American Gin; Krogstad Festlig Aquavit; The Stillroom series of limited, small-batch spirits; Volstead Vodka
Address: 2025 SE 7th Avenue, Portland, OR 97214
Web: housespirits.com

New Deal Distillery

Another of Portland's wave of pioneering distillers, the New Deal Distillery, founded by Matthew VanWinkle and Tom Burkleaux, has been crafting its wares since 2004. With New Deal Vodka and Portland 88 Vodka as the crowning glories of its liquor stash, these guys focus on getting the perfect cut of spirits from their small still set-up, tasting each batch as it runs off in order to get the real heart of the liquor.

Craft spirits: New Deal 33 Portland Dry Gin; New Deal Gin No. 1; Coffee Liqueur; Ginger Liqueur; Hot Monkey Vodka; Mud Puddle Chocolate Vodka; New Deal Vodka; Portland 88 Vodka
Address: 900 SE Salmon Street, Portland, OR 97214
Web: newdealdistillery.com

Rolling River Spirits

A relative newbie on the block, RRS—founded in 2011—proudly bills itself as a family-run set-up. The Rickards, who small-batch distill their wheat-and-rye-based spirit, are currently only producing a vodka—but, good things come to those who wait, and a whiskey is on the cards in the not-too-distant future.

Craft spirits: Rolling River Vodka, Rolling River Whiskey (coming soon), Rolling River Gin (coming sooner)
Address: 1215 SE 8th Avenue, Suite H, Portland, OR 97214
Web: rollingriverspirits.com

Stone Barn Brandyworks

Proving that no niche is too small in the world of craft spirits, Sebastian and Erika Degens use the seasonal fruits in Oregon to distill their sensational Cranberry Liqueur, among other tempting fruit brandies. It's an according-to-market set-up, so, in winter, when there's nothing on the trees to distill, they turn their hand to whiskey-making. A selection of different wood finishes adds another element of interest to the operation.

Craft spirits: Changing seasonal spirits; Cranberry Liqueur; Red Wing Coffee Liqueur; Easy Eight Unoaked Oat Whiskey; Hard Eight Unoaked Rye Whiskey; Hoppin' Eights Aged Whiskey
Address: 3315 SE 19th Avenue, Suite B, Portland, OR 97202
Web: stonebarnbrandyworks.com

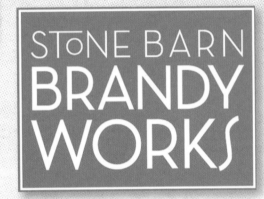

Vinn Distillery

Another family distillery, this time with the USP that the recipes used have been followed by the Ly family for generations, handed down as their forebears moved from China to Vietnam, and eventually to the USA. Vinn vodka was a first in America, being produced from rice as its base organic material. *Baijiu* (pronounced "bye-joe") is a traditional Chinese white liquor that is typically drunk with food.

Craft spirits: Baijiu Vodka; Mijiu Fire; Mijiu Ice
Address: 833 SE Main Street, Suite 125, Portland, OR 97214
Web: vinndistillery.com

SO, WHAT ACTUALLY IS CRAFT DISTILLING?

No matter who you ask in the craft spirit world, this seemingly straightforward question is usually met with a furrowed brow and a politician's answer. For our purposes, a working definition could be along the lines of: a person or a bunch of people who—in pursuit of the dream of excellent booze—turn organic matter into delicious-tasting alcohol. Certainly, the romantic might like to think of these charmingly amateur operations as having been spawned from a mad-cap individual's dream and realized in a garden shed, but, in reality, there are plenty of gray areas where "craft" and "commercial" can look pretty similar. So, for a more accurate definition we are going to have to dig a little deeper and explore a few additional factors, some more tangible than others...

DOES SIZE MATTER?

Tom Mooney, the first President of the American Craft Distilling Association (ACDA), has spent more time than most thinking about what "craft distilling" is (after all, the definition governs membership of the association). Picking his brains raised some interesting points: craft, Tom says, is about scale, independence, and honesty. Very nice—except that including "scale" as part of your definition of craft is inherently problematic. Those distillers who started out with a bathtub-scale production, but became hugely successful, are at risk of getting booted out of their own movement should they choose to upsize production to meet growing demand.

For the ACDA, though, a fixed upper-output restriction is key. "We think that limiting the size of production is important, not least because it limits the resources you have," says Tom. "Of course, large companies can turn out all sorts of great products—but we believe there are some things that you just cannot produce on a big, global scale. I'm not just talking quirks in the spirit, but real, tangible things that end up affecting the consumer experience. Scale isn't just how many cases you turn out, but it's about how you make the product; there is a very substantial difference between making gin in a pot still a few cases at a time and flavoring gin off a column still in very large quantities."

Can "craft" be big?

Of course, there is a huge difference between large-scale, commercial column stills and small-scale pot stills (and more on this later), but is this reason enough on its own to limit a distillery's production? There are interesting parallels with the beer world, where the definition of a "craft brewery" is theoretically limited to the size of the Boston Beer Company that year, and, as the firm grows, this gets adjusted up. "This eventually starts to feel disingenuous," Tom points out. "Especially when you are looking at multi-billion dollar companies and beer billionaires."

Admittedly, multi-billion dollar operations don't sound very craft—they are certainly a long way from that garden-shed mentality—but is slapping a limit on the output of a craft distillery actually practical? To avoid eliminating too many of its members, the ACDA has already had to revise the limit that it puts on production upward—it has been raised from 50,000 2-gallon/9-liter cases a year to 750,000 proof gallons or 400,000 cases—and admits that this could well be reviewed in the future.

Interestingly, on the other side of the pond, spirits writer and the founder of the Craft Distillers' Alliance, Dominic Roskrow, is quick to rule out "scale" as a criterion. "In America, you can't be a craft distiller once you become a big organization—but that means, as soon as anybody becomes too successful, we've got to kick them out of the alliance. So, craft can't necessarily be about size," he says.

Although scale is pleasingly quantifiable, we won't be ruling producers in or out on the basis of a maximum size. There are other more important factors, such as individuality and integrity, to take into account in this book...

STICKING IT TO THE MAN

Let's look at the question of independence: we should be on pretty safe ground including this as a vital criterion for craft; it is, after all, a counter-conventional movement, disassociated from what the establishment is doing. The new craft distillers are proud to be different—making a product that they believe in and to hell with the risks and the rules and the conventions. Craft should feel both artisan and also a little renegade: no one is saying these craft distillers are doing things better than the industry's big boys (and there is more on this question of quality later), but they are sure as heck doing things their own way.

Back to Tom Mooney, who says: "Independence is very important—not just because it defines who we are as companies, but also because it's an indicator of people's willingness to take risks. We are able to do things with traditional categories that revolutionizes

them and which larger companies wouldn't do. There's a certain spirit of entrepreneurship that comes with being a smaller producer. The cynic might argue that this is because we have got a lot less to lose, but the fact is a lot of the innovation and a lot of the changes we're pioneering in the categories don't come from the top down; they come from the craft producers and move up."

Is it as black and white as that, though? Consider the small-batch, single-malt Scotch distiller who malts his own barley, ferments it, pot-distils, and then ages it on a remote island, before cutting it with pure mountain water and packing it for market. So far, so craft—yes? But, what if the backing for that same distiller came from a large, faceless industry giant—does that mean what the distiller is doing is no longer craft because he's on a corporation's payroll? For the moment, we should argue that it does. We want our craft distillers to be free to do what they want, and not hampered by limitations or regulations placed on them by an anonymous head office. But watch this space. The business sharks are circling around many independents and, should your favorite craft brand get swallowed up, you may find yourself feeling differently.

THE INTEGRITY OF CRAFT

The third and final criterion that Tom names for the ACDA's craft distillers is "honesty"—an interesting and important one. "Asking our members to sign up to a code of honesty differs from anything that is going on in the beer market," says Mooney. "Can someone really look at a bottle and tell what's in it? We want the answer to that to be 'yes'... We think it's extremely important that the labeling explains exactly what's in the bottle; how it was produced; and where it's from—the crafted brand, not the crafty brand." This hints at a rather grubby element of the craft movement, which we do need to address: not all spirits that are packaged as "craft" have had anything to do with small-scale distillation. While, in an ideal world, we would hope that all craft distillers had lovingly raised their own barley, herded their own dairy cows, or tilled the land to grow their own potatoes, before taking that organic product, fermenting it, and then distilling it, the reality is somewhat different.

Instead, many "craft" producers skip this first step by buying in a neutral-grain spirit that they then flavor and package as required. Close your eyes and picture a craft spirit bottle—it's got an unconventional bottle shape, right? An artfully designed label with fonts that convey a certain message of individuality and authenticity, provenance and independence, and so on... We "know" intuitively what a craft bottle looks like—so, too, do those less salubrious characters who imitate the look of craft, but without any of the artisan processes behind it. It's perfectly legal to use words such as "artisan" or "craft" on the bottle, no matter whether the product truly is craft. The key to the future is transparency about what's going into the bottle. Consumers need to know what they're buying: craft-a-likes or the genuine article.

Having the right approach

Dominic Roskrow goes further: "To me, it's about attitude—it's fantastic that we're seeing this movement, but, if you look at, for example, all those independent gins in the store, the vast majority of them come from one base source; in the case of gin, they're not actually distilling at all, they are rectifying—adding the botanicals and doing a second distillation for which you don't need a distiller's licence. Done without transparency, and without integrity, there's a lot of packaging and not necessarily a lot of crafting going on."

So, back to the imperfect definition of a craft distiller: a person or bunch of people who—in pursuit of the dream of excellent booze—turn organic matter into delicious-tasting alcohol. We can now elaborate on this to be a bit more precise: an independent person or bunch of people who—in pursuit of the dream of excellent booze—produce artisan alcohol, and represent their processes fairly and accurately to the consumer.

At its roots, craft distilling is about integrity—in the ingredients, the process, the philosophy, and the end result. If what's in the bottle tastes good, then that's even better.

LIQUID ALCHEMY: WHAT IS DISTILLING?

Understanding a little about the actual process of distilling will help you make more informed choices about the booze you are buying. If, for example, you have no idea of the difference between a pot or a column still, then how are you meant to know what small-batch actually means? So, back to school—here comes the basics.

FIRST, SELECT YOUR BASE ELEMENT

Pretty much anything on your weekly shopping list (such as apples, potatoes, grapes, cereal, and even milk) can be converted into something fit for your liquor cabinet. If sugar already exists naturally in your selected material—the fructose in fruit, for example—then you can crack on and get fermenting. Grain, on the other hand, needs a little encouragement to get things going—which is where "malting" comes in (as in "malted barley"). This is essentially a process by which water and warmth are applied to the grain to encourage germination; this makes the starches in the grain soluble so that they can be lured out and dissolved in water. The grain is then crushed and mashed up with hot water so that the starches dissolve and form a lovely, warm soup, in which the enzymes busily work to convert the starches into sugar. This sugar soup (which is actually called a wort) is now ripe and ready for fermentation, in much the same way as your grape or apple juice.

The fermentation process is a relatively simple one—the sugar-rich liquid is combined with yeast (which can either be naturally occurring or introduced by the distiller). The yeast gobbles up the sugars and, in doing so, produces carbon dioxide (as a by-product) and alcohol (ethanol—AKA the good bit). By the time the yeast has had its fill, the resulting liquid, which is called a wash, should be around 10% alcohol.

NEXT UP, MAKE IT STRONGER

Now comes the bit we're really interested in: how to turn what is basically cider, beer, or wine, etc.—depending on your base material—into good hard liquor. So, the fundamental principle of distilling is this: our wash is essentially made up of water and ethanol, plus a few all-important flavor compounds and a very few other alcohol nasties. These components have different boiling temperatures—water's obviously being 212°F (100°C), while ethanol's (the bit we want) is around 72°F (22°C) lower. To separate the boozy bit from the H_2O, the distiller heats up the liquid until the components he wants begin to vaporize; this vapor is cooled, condensed, and collected. It becomes, in its new form, a more alcoholic and flavorful product.

That's the nuts and bolts of the process, but the specific type of still you use (i.e. either a pot or a continuous still) requires variations in the production process that have a huge impact on the nature of the spirit you're going to produce. This is extremely relevant to the craft distiller who—almost always—will want to small-batch produce using a pot still.

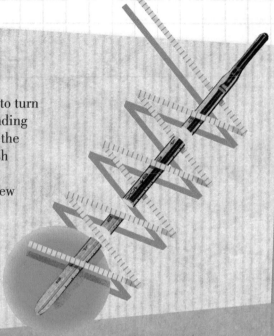

QUIRKY AND CHARACTERFUL POT DISTILLATION

When most people picture a still—that shiny, copper kettle affair with a swooping neck— what they are thinking of is a pot still. Aside from a few premium producers and the Scotch industry, this is becoming increasingly rare in the commercial spirit world. A pot still is the oldest type of still, and the one most suited to the craft process, because it promotes character and makes a genuinely consistent product hard to achieve. If you're using a pot still, then you are "batch-distilling"—i.e. you cook up one load of booze at a time. However, because the design of the pot still is not the most efficient, a couple of distillations (often done with two different stills) will be required to get the liquid to a high enough alcohol percentage. If you're making single malt whisky, the first of these stills is called a wash still, and the second, which is smaller, is known as a spirit still.

What's the pot still made from?

If there's enough cash to fund it, pot stills are often made from copper—not because they look good (though they undoubtedly do)—but because copper is a highly malleable metal and so can be manipulated to make the main pot and its swan's neck to precise designs. It's also another element that adds character, as the spirit interacts with the metal. Along the way, and through the years, a few dents and quirks appear in copper stills, and you'll find distillers tend to talk about them as if they are cantankerous elderly relatives or temperamental cars: each has its foibles, and personality (and, of course, a name)—but treat 'em right, and they'll run sweetly.

Every still is different

Because of the way the evaporation process works, the size and shape of the still—and, in particular, its neck—have a surprisingly big impact on the spirit you're producing. Short necks tend to produce robust spirits, while long ones give more elegant flavors. (Chances are, this means that the character of your favorite Scotch came about by accident rather than design, thanks to whatever shape of pot still the distillery's forefathers happened to have fashioned.) But, now we understand why this happens: in stills with very tall necks, the heavier components of the vapor, which have the highest boiling points, will cool, condense, and drop back into the still, rather than pass through the neck to be collected. Rather unattractively, this is called reflux. Despite sounding like a digestive disorder, this is a useful process, as many of these heavier alcohols give less than pleasant flavors and textures to the spirit. If, on the other hand, your swan's neck is more akin to a duck, and your still is on the rotund side, you'll most likely produce robust and flavorful spirits—since they don't have as far to travel, those heavy alcohol and flavor molecules are able to stay suspended in vapor long enough to make it onto the condensing side of the still.

Getting to the good stuff

So, here is a key to the pot-distiller's art—whatever shape of still you are dealing with, the science stays the same: the lightest, most volatile elements of the wash, which contain lighter flavor compounds (such as florals) will vaporize first; the heaviest (which have the

most intense flavors, eventually becoming impure and unpleasant) will vaporize last. The really good stuff—the heart of the spirit, which is known as the cut—comes in the middle of the evaporation process. No distiller wants the heads (the first bit of vapor to come over) or the tails (the last), as these are full of unpleasant flavors and compounds (not to mention methanol). However, selecting which portion of the ethanol-rich, desirable soul of the spirit to take relies on the distiller's nose and instinct. The narrower the cut the distiller takes (and, therefore, the amount of product he or she is willing to discard), then the more precise and high-quality the spirit.

COLUMN STILLS
(AKA THE INDUSTRIAL REVOLUTION)

In the 18th century, deep in County Cork, Ireland, a cry of "Eureka" could (probably) be heard as one Sir Anthony Perrier completed his plans for the column still. Though it was later to be modified by a Scot, Robert Stein, and another Irishman, Aeneas Coffey—who both lent their names to their interpretations—it was Perrier's design that fundamentally changed the distilling industry. Eliminating the need for "batch distilling" with those cranky, old, size-limited pot stills, Perrier's column stills, and the continuous still that followed, became a means to produce totally consistent spirit, with no need to stop distilling, until either your warehouses were overflowing or your ingredients had dried up. Doubtless, a few lone voices howled into the storm that it was a shame to lose the character from the spirit—as well as the charm of slight variations from batch to batch that a pot still could give—but it would have been like proclaiming the virtues of a horse and cart over the motor car: efficient, fast, and with seemingly limitless capacity, supporters of the column still were convinced it was the future. And they were right.

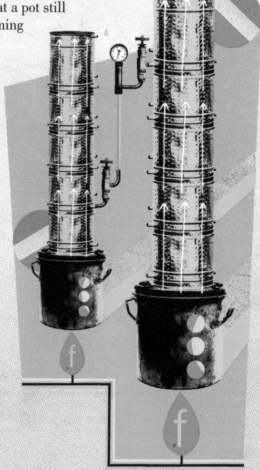

Understanding the science

So, how does this revolutionary beast work? Well, remember with pot distillation how we either needed two stills, or to run the distillation a number of times, to get the required level of rectified alcohol? The column still does away with this stage by running a series of fractional (micro-) distillations at the same time, separating the fermented liquid extremely precisely into its different components. Picture a large tube, with layers of hole-studded plates stacked up inside it, and a pipe coming into the bottom and another at the top. The heated vapor hisses into the bottom of the still and passes up through the layers of plates; as with a pot still, the higher the vapor rises, the more it cools, and so those parts of the wash with higher boiling temperatures drop down onto the plates. Once a plate is full up, any additional vapor condensing into liquid at that level will have to overflow onto the one below, where it heats up again, and the process is repeated on a micro-scale. While hundreds of micro-distillations are taking place on each plate, overall the most volatile components—including ethanol—are working their way up to the top of the still where the most highly rectified spirit sits. The distiller is able to judge in which trays different "fractions" of the distillation are, and can run off the components he wants using a series of taps.

But is it "craft"?

This kind of still can run and run, as long as you have enough fermented liquid to feed in (and enough room for the spirit you produce), but the new-make spirit that comes off a column still, though available in ready quantities and of a consistent quality, lacks the nuanced flavor of a pot-still distillate. This is not to say that column stills cannot be used in craft—on the contrary, they are a traditional way to distill spirits such as bourbon and Armagnac—but, the vast majority of them are found on huge scales in commercial operations, with tall towers and a multitude of columns, which means that the alcohol becomes purer and purer (and, conversely, less and less characterful).

No matter which kind of still you are running, the rectified new-make spirit you collect—whether you're producing whiskey, brandy, or gin—will be clear, strong, and relatively characterless (i.e. vodka). A few more processes lie ahead of the liquor as it makes its way to the bottle, including—for gin—a close encounter with some botanicals, and for darker spirits, maturation and blending.

WOOD:
THE VITAL INGREDIENT

Without wood, there would be no whiskey (a sobering thought). In fact, for any dark spirit, distillation is just the start of a long, gentle journey toward the bottle—during which it must spend an awkward adolescence having its personality rounded by a number of years in barrel. The type of wood used, the size and age of the barrel, and the climate of the warehouse—hell, even its position on the shelves—will have a significant impact on the clear, new-make spirit that splashed off the still. In fact, up to 70 percent of the character of a dark spirit comes from its wood.

The wood gives the spirit color, as well as flavor, and—vitally—allows it to mature in a porous environment, with some components evaporating away (the notorious "angel's share") and others mellowing through contact with air. As a rule of thumb, the newer the wood, the more flavor it will impart to the spirit—expect vanilla (if it is aged in oak) and spices, along with some nutty and fruity elements, too. Some barrels will be toasted before they're filled —which literally involves charring them over a flame— and these, as you would expect, also give smoky, caramelized flavors.

The investment in wood—and, in fact, in the whole aging process—is hugely expensive for distillers, and so it is no surprise that many craft distillers who are just starting out tend to favor vodka, gin, and other unaged spirits that require little or no time in costly barrels. We'll touch more on the specifics of wood in the dark spirit chapters.

AND FINALLY: THE BLEND

Whether the spirit is aged or not, the distillers have another job to do before it can be bottled: blending. For the craft distiller, who is trying to promote individual, batch-to-batch quirks, this is less relevant, but for anyone hoping to achieve a "house-style" blend, it is vital. When making aged spirits, the blending process can even out any quirks which have developed over time, and, with a number of barrels at his or her disposal, the distiller can use different ingredients to create a consistent product.

Lastly, before the spirit can be bottled, the rectified alcohol content needs to be brought down to a sensible drinking percentage—a process that is usually done using pure, demineralized water. While at this stage commercial distillers would usually chill-filter their product to remove any unwanted color or character, the very thought of this is usually enough to bring craft distillers out in a cold sweat: after all, preserving character is the essence of what they are about. Now, the bottling line awaits.

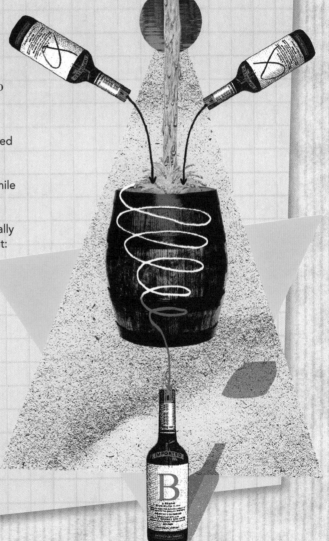

Part 2

HOW TO TASTE SPIRITS

You may be thinking that this is a chapter worth skipping—after all, you know how tasting works: simply transport liquid to mouth, sip, swallow, and then make appreciative (or other) noises. But, when it comes to craft spirits, being able to taste effectively and assess the real quality of what you're drinking is vital. Where the big commercial boys are continuously and rigorously quality controlled—no matter what that quality is—and are expected to output a consistent product, the same cannot be said for the craft spirit world. This, friends, is the Wild West—and you need to know how to spot the cowboys, as well as when you've struck distilling gold.

GETTING STARTED

The first thing to be said is that trying to assess the quality of anything independently of expectation, presentation, and packaging is practically impossible. For example, if you pour wine into black glassware, consumers can struggle to identify red from white. Tell people that one product is more premium than another, and sub-conscious parts of the brain swing into action, making it impossible for them to assess it impartially. Neuro-economist Baba Shiv, Director of the Strategic Marketing Management Executive Program at Stanford, recently conducted an experiment whereby test subjects were asked to sample five different wines, which they were told cost between $5 and $90. The wines were presented in a random order and the subjects were told the value of each sample before tasting it. Their brain activity was monitored throughout. Interestingly, no matter in which price order they sampled the wines, there was lots more activity in the part of the brain coded for pleasure when they were tasting the $90 bottle. The trick—if you haven't guessed already—was that, unbeknownst to the subjects, each of the five samples they tasted was exactly the same wine.

ASSESSING SPIRITS

"There is a correlation between price and quality," Baba explains. "There is an expectation that high price equals high quality; so, what is effectively happening is a price placebo effect: the higher expectations that come with the higher price turn into a self-fulfilling prophecy. The brain actually does extract more pleasure from the high-price wines than when it thinks it is tasting low-priced wines." So, although the product was identical throughout, those wines believed to be more premium actually tasted better to the test subjects.

As consumers, how can we stop our treacherous brains from leaping ahead and over-riding our efforts to judge a spirit objectively? Ideally, we would always assess a spirit "blind"—with the style, packaging, and price concealed—but this is rarely possible. After all, assuming you bought the bottle you're about to taste, you've already made certain assumptions about the product based on its aesthetics, reputation, and context. However, there are a few useful steps you can take to try to stave off preconceptions (conscious or otherwise).

Firstly, get a notebook to record tastings as you go along—writing down your impressions helps you formulate an opinion of the spirit, putting the flavors into words, and helps to calibrate your palate. Some people are especially sensitive to bitter flavors, others to the sensation of alcohol—once you've recorded a few spirits, you will begin to see if there are trends emerging in what and how you taste. We also want to introduce a little method to the madness—guidelines, not rules, of course—and work through the different aspects of a spirit: how it smells, how it tastes, and that all-important judgment of how good it really is.

POURING A TASTING SAMPLE

No matter whether you are a water-in-your-whiskey (or a tonic-in-your-gin-or-vodka) kind of character, you need to sample a spirit neat if you are to taste it properly. Industry professionals say that around 11 o'clock in the morning is the best time to crack open a bottle, as your sensory faculties are at their sharpest then—although a pre-lunchtime tipple could raise a few eyebrows among concerned friends and family. Tasting neat obviously means you'll be supping liquor that's very high in alcohol, so be aware that your palate can quickly get fatigued and be sure to take a break long before your tongue starts to go numb. Also, keep water to hand in order to cleanse your palate when required. Whether you choose to spit or swallow is entirely down to personal preference.

Keep it clean

You should also practice good tasting hygiene: this doesn't involve taking a shower before you get started (although…), but rather means that you want to approach the glass free of other sensory distractions: so, no strong fragrances, no lingering tastes in your mouth (avoid coffee, curry, garlic, and so on in the hours running up to a tasting), and try to avoid having any diverting odors such as air freshener in the room, or embarking on a tasting with someone who is trial-running the Lynx effect.

A respectable receptacle

Next up, you want a tasting glass. The ideal size and shape for tasting is a small wine glass, rather than a classic whiskey tumbler (for the ones the pros use, Google "ISO tasting glass"). This is going to let you get a good noseful of the aromas, trapping them rather than allowing them to escape into the ether, as they would in a straight-sided glass. Once you've sourced your chosen vessel, consider using it for all future tasting escapades, so that you can compare and contrast consistently—you'll be amazed at the impact a differently shaped glass can have on your perception of an alcohol.

So—at last—let's open the bottle and pour a decent measure of spirit. Stick to a barman's serving of 1.7fl oz (50ml), so that you're able to give it a good swirl without slopping it all over yourself or the sofa. (Once your clothes start smelling of booze, people will inevitably ask questions.)

JUDGING BY APPEARANCES

Find yourself a sheet of white paper or a white tablecloth so that you have a solid, plain background against which to get a decent look at the liquid and eye up its color and clarity. This is your first chance to check for irregularities, features, or faults. While, commercially, most spirits are filtered (and will say so on the bottle) to remove any impurities—a process which will be repeated multiple times for, say, vodka—you may see a haze of sediment suspended in the liquid with craft bottles, especially if it is a bit cold. This is because these impurities often translate to flavor congeners, color, and character, which crafties are looking to preserve in order to create an idiosyncratic product. In the mainstream marketplace, small-batch, single-malt whiskies are often un-chill-filtered for this self-same reason. Be aware, though, that if a degree of cloudiness in the spirit isn't deliberate (i.e. where the spirit has been filtered, but particles remain), this could indicate a fault.

Setting the tone

The color of the liquid can also give you a few clues about what's in the glass—anything tap-water clear is likely to be totally unaged; conversely, the darker a spirit gets, the more wood it is likely to have seen. But, beware the false friends: you need to keep in mind that filtration can remove color, while additives, such as caramel, can be used to create a warmer color.

After you've looked for clarity and color, give the glass a good swirl again and hold it up to the light. Check out what kind of legs (or "tears") the spirit has—these are the rivulets of liquid that form on the sides of the glass. The legs indicate both alcohol and sugar content: the more pronounced they are, the more alcohol, sugar, or both, the spirit contains. Sherlock-like, you should have formed an initial impression by now—so, let's see if your deductions are borne out.

STICK YOUR BEAK IN

Your nose is a faithful ally in assessing a spirit's quality. Give the glass a good swirl to get the liquid moving around—this will help release the flavor aromas—then stick your nose in there and take a short, sharp sniff. The first—and quite possibly the most overwhelming—impression will probably be a hit of alcohol, especially if you are particularly sensitive to it. If this is all you get from a first smell, then wait a second and get back in there for another go: what you are looking for is a sense of the bouquet's concentration and intensity. While you're unlikely to get much from vodka, you should get a truck-load of intensity from, say, a peated whisky.

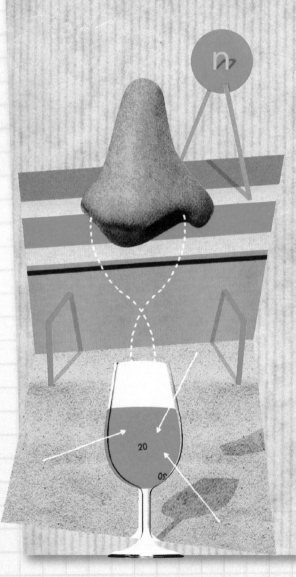

Looking for clues

Next up, you want to see whether there are any clues in there about how the spirit has been made: oak-aging, for example, can be detected by smells akin to vanilla ice cream and coconut, while, if you start to pick up on Christmas-cake flavors—stewed fruit, spice, raisins, and so on—then you are likely to be looking at a more mature drop.

Jot down any aromas that jump out of the glass—these can be entirely wacky and personal ("the polish on my school hall floor" or "great Aunt Edna's rock cakes" etc.), or you can try and stick in the realm of convention and go with florals, fruit, cereals, woods, spices, herbs, dairy, and so on. More unusual aromas, such as rubber, leather, antiseptic, gravy, and even petrol, could well be in there, so relax and write down anything and everything that springs to mind. Go back to it a couple of times: different things may jump out the glass. If your nose is becoming anesthetized, sniff the back of your hand—this will "recalibrate" it so that you're good for a few more sniffs.

AND FINALLY...

Now for the good bit: tasting. There are a few boxes we want to tick here, in terms of judging what's in the glass, the first of which is sweetness. Science says we're biologically programmed to pick up—and perhaps even to seek out—sweetness. Whether that's because of the lactose in human milk or the fact that, in nature, sweetness indicates calories (and calories mean survival), it doesn't much matter; what we need to know is that evolution has dictated sugar to be one of the first "taste" elements that we register and is generally detected on the tip of the tongue.

Sugar levels

So, how sweet is the spirit? Can you hear the distant whine of the dentist's drill and is your enamel aching? Or, on the other hand, is it practically lip-smackingly savory? Try and judge out of 10, from *umami* at one end of the scale to full-on liquid glucose at the other. The level of sweetness can be translated into some useful information about the spirit: once fermentation and distillation have happened, spirits don't contain any sugar, so any sweetness you're detecting has either been added by the producer, post-distillation, or has come from contact with wood.

Next up, we want to feel the burn—which is how the level of alcohol is usually perceived. Are your gums being stripped raw by rubbing alcohol, or is this more of a well-rounded, smooth warmth? In general, unaged or badly made spirits will taste as though they contain a lot more alcohol because of this burn factor. More aged and mellow spirits—or those that have been very highly filtered to remove any impurities—have a less astringent effect on your mouth. (The actual ABV could be identical, but it is important to judge how well-integrated the alcohol is.) The combined effect of the sugar and alcohol levels in the spirit gives you a sense of "weight" (AKA mouthfeel or body). Is your spirit a full-bodied, oily beast? A creamy, silky one? Or an ephemeral, whisper-light one?

Last, but not least, dust off your imagination and vocabulary (or just use the flavor wheel over the page) to try to lock down the flavors you experience when sipping. You'll find that different points of the "taste"—first impression, middle of the palate, and finish—will give you different characteristics. Try to put all your impressions into words—animal, vegetable, or mineral—to get a solid sense of what you're drinking. If you've only managed to rustle up a couple of descriptors, it's fair to say that the spirit is pretty simple. If, on the other hand, you've just noted down a Pulitzer-worthy paragraph, then give this spirit plenty of credit as "complex."

This brings us to your final task—the purpose of our exercise—to form an overall judgment of whether this is a decent-quality drop. So, disregarding how it was packaged, or how much of a hit your credit card took to buy it, does the liquid in the glass stand up to close examination? Was it clear? Did it have an interesting and evocative nose? Did it have an appealing body and texture? And did it taste good?

Hopefully, the answer to all of the above is a resounding "yes."

FLAVOR WHEEL

Use the flavor wheel below as a guide to understanding the tastes and flavors you will experience when sampling different spirits.

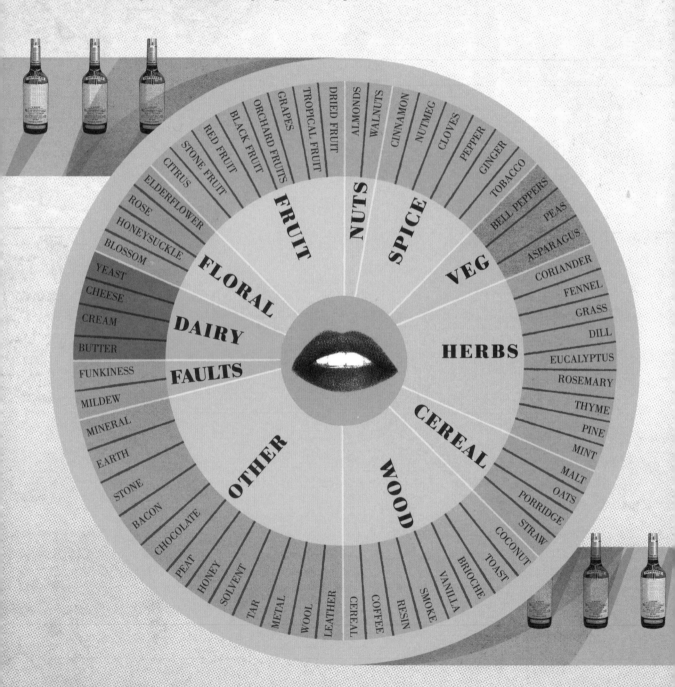

FRUIT
NUTS
SPICE
VEG
FLORAL
HERBS
DAIRY
FAULTS
OTHER
CEREAL
WOOD

DRIED FRUIT
TROPICAL FRUIT
GRAPES
ORCHARD FRUITS
BLACK FRUIT
RED FRUIT
STONE FRUIT
CITRUS
ELDERFLOWER
ROSE
HONEYSUCKLE
BLOSSOM
YEAST
CHEESE
CREAM
BUTTER
FUNKINESS
MILDEW
MINERAL
EARTH
STONE
BACON
CHOCOLATE
PEAT
HONEY
SOLVENT
TAR
METAL
WOOL
LEATHER
CEREAL
COFFEE
RESIN
SMOKE
VANILLA
BRIOCHE
TOAST
COCONUT
STRAW
PORRIDGE
OATS
MALT
MINT
PINE
THYME
ROSEMARY
EUCALYPTUS
DILL
GRASS
FENNEL
CORIANDER
ASPARAGUS
PEAS
BELL PEPPERS
TOBACCO
GINGER
PEPPER
CLOVES
NUTMEG
CINNAMON
WALNUTS
ALMONDS

AND FINALLY (PART II):
A NOTE FROM THE AUTHOR

Taste is subjective. One of the best things about really enjoying food and drink—whether you're tucking into an artisan product or a store-bought favorite—is that there are no wrong answers when it comes to what's good. If you rate it, then that's all that matters. Without doubt, some of the most enjoyable drinks I've had the pleasure of sampling tasted especially delicious because of the excellent company in which they were served, or because the weather that day really suited them—little can touch a good, peaty single malt on a storm-lashed, day or an elegant rosé when the sun's beating down and there's an ocean view—or because the combination with a particular food just worked.

For me, good drinks and good times are inextricably linked; my favorite brands are invariably those that I enjoyed, not just in the clinical environs of a tasting room, but also in great bars, in great restaurants, and with great friends. With that in mind—and especially considering the vast scope of our subject matter—I have to apologize if your favorite craft brand hasn't been included in these pages. Those that I have picked out have been selected because, for me—judged as objectively as possible on the merits of what's in the bottle—they taste superb; they represent good value when it comes to the impact on your wallet; they are of good quality; and they are made by crazily enthusiastic and seriously talented people who care—really care—about craft.

Part 3

THE BEST DISTILLERS IN THE WORLD

Like great wine or beer, these craft spirits have a terroir: they encapsulate the ingredients and character of the place in which they were created. They're products of quality rather than quantity. Artisan spirits can not only taste better, but each micro-distiller has a tale to tell about the ingredients or the dream that lead them to lovingly coax each drop of spirit from still to bottle. Here are those stories.

VODKA

On the grand and glorious scale of alcohol, with its myriad styles and flavors of liquor, vodka is zero. It is Alpha, neutral; nothing but a base spirit. In fact, especially with most commercial iterations, its inherent nothingness—or purity—is extolled as a virtue ("Filtered through lava!" "Made from icebergs!"). However, this doesn't mean that it should be dismissed out of hand as an alcoholic persona non grata, especially when it comes to craft.

LOOKING FOR CLUES

If you consider that vodka is simply ethanol and water, then the degrees of flavor variance we are talking about are minimal. Most flavor and color compounds are stripped out to leave behind a spirit that can certainly have textural variation and, once your palate is tuned in, some taste differentials. However, the more artisan your production method, the more character is likely to slip through the net or be actively encouraged, i.e. in crafted spirits, where the production processes are not aligned with ultra-precise industrial standards, you may actually get a spirit that tastes a lot more interesting than something which has been column-distilled and charcoal-filtered. You may not, of course, but that's all part of the fun.

Keeping it neutral

When it comes to the key ingredient for vodka, the fundamental rule is pretty much this: if it grows, you can distil it—any fermentable natural material, from grapes to grain, milk to molasses, is fair game. Right from the get-go in the production process, vodka makers are looking to minimize flavor congeners rather than encourage them (as, say, a whiskey distiller might do), and so everything about the process seeks to promote alcoholic strength and purity. As a general rule, grain vodkas tend to be the higher-quality ones, while vodkas made from potatoes are creamier in texture, and anything made using molasses is probably down the lower-quality end of the spectrum.

As with any liquor, step one is to kick off fermentation in order to make the wash/beer/wine. When making vodka, this is often done by adding enzymes to encourage the process, while also controlling any rogue flavor elements (such as those which might creep in on a traditional Scotch malting floor, for example), though many craft distillers go to great lengths to keep things as natural as possible. The wash is then distilled and rectified, often several times, especially if a pot still is being used, because there are legal minimum requirements regarding the strength of around 95% proof plus that needs to be achieved for vodka. Some producers will proudly display on the label the number of times their vodka has been distilled, though chances are this has been done for reasons of necessity rather than stylistic preference.

Before bottling, the high-strength ethanol is commonly filtered through charcoal, lava, silver, platinum—you name it—to remove any impurities, as well as color and flavour compounds. This stops the vodka going cloudy if it is chilled, so, if yours is unfiltered, some haze at low temperatures is nothing to worry about. Finally, the spirit needs to be brought down to a less cirrhosis-inducing percentage, and so it is cut with water. The water used is a key ingredient, so the source, as well as how it's treated, is an important consideration: usually, it will be demineralized to minimize any potential intrusions of flavor.

Tastes as good as it looks?

Once the vodka has been bottled next comes arguably the biggest factor that influences the flavor and aroma… the packaging. Of course, there is a discernible difference between the type of vodka consumed on park benches and that which commands substantial prices and has been made with an emphasis on quality, but, undoubtedly, in the vodka category more than any other, the narrative on the bottle and the packaging itself will influence your impression of what lies within. Could you, hand on heart, really tell the difference between two top-notch brands, say Grey Goose and Belvedere, if you were blindfolded? What about if they had a mixer in them? Exactly.

A NOTE ON THE VODKAS

When selecting which distilleries to include, precedence and preference have been given to those producers who are "grain (or potato or grape) to glass" over those who simply re-distil and package their wares. This seems especially pertinent in the vodka category, where neither botanicals nor aging are involved, and the true craft comes from the sourcing of the materials, their fermentation, and, finally, their distillation. These things combine to give you flavorful, interesting spirits, so prepare for your tastebuds to be tangled with.

Woody Creek Signature Potato Vodka (40% abv)

WOODY CREEK DISTILLERS, COLORADO, USA

• Grand Teton   • Cold River

Woody Creek •   • Leopold Bros

What do you get if you cross a NASA engineer with a Rio Grande potato and two 34ft (10m) rectifying stills? The answer, as you may have guessed, is a premium craft vodka—and a pretty unique one at that—not only because it is made from potatoes, but also because Woody Creek manages the entire production process, from planting the crops to filling the bottles, eschewing the more common practice of buying in neutral grain alcohol.

Three friends: husband-and-wife team Mary and Pat Scanlan (the latter being the space engineer), along with Colorado-based businessman Mark Kleckner, set up their impressive CARL Distilling System in the eponymous Woody Creek in 2012.

At the turn of the 20th century, when silver-hunters were crawling over the state, Colorado was famed for its potato production. Mary and Pat decided to turn their family farm over to reviving this tradition, planting 30 acres (12 hectares) with historic potato varieties. They concluded that Rio Grande had the flavorful, starchy characteristics they were looking for and so majored on its production. Around Labor Day each year, come harvest time, tonnes of potatoes make their way into a brewer's mash within 48 hours of coming out of the earth for maximum flavor, liquid, and freshness.

The still set-up is such that the spirit only needs be distilled once in order to meet the legal requisite strength, which is an advantage over those who have to run numerous distillations, says Kleckner, as it allows more flavor to be retained in the spirit. It's unfiltered, and nothing—other than, of course, demineralized water from the Rocky Mountains—is added: its mouthfeel and flavor all come from potato-based goodness.

Tasting notes: Almost crème brûlée, with a dairy sweetness on the nose and a smooth, mouth-filling palate, along with a whiff of sharp spice (pepper) and a herbal note akin to rosemary, make this a delicious sipping vodka, or rather good in a martini.

Price: $$

Other products: Woody Creek Reserve Stobrawa Vodka (made with a starchy Polish potato); a whiskey is in the pipeline for release in 2015.

Web: woodycreekdistillers.com

Cold River Vodka (40% ABV)

MAINE DISTILLERIES, MAINE, USA

The question of what to do with an ugly potato keeps few of us awake at night (is there actually such a thing as a good-looking potato?), but for Don Thibodeau, who headed up Green Thumb Farm in Maine, the idea of turning aesthetically challenged Norwis white spuds into a rather beautiful vodka had obvious appeal.

The seed of the idea had been sown years before: Don, the fifth generation of a potato-farming family, had grown up listening to his father Larry holding forth about distilling potatoes during the Prohibition era. Spurred on, not only by the thought that the potato wastage could be reduced, but also because a drop in potato prices could be offset, Cold River (named after the distillery's water source) was founded in 2006.

The operation inaugurated by Don and a handful of friends and family (Chris, Joe, Matt, Ben, Bob, and Lee) was a far cry from the bootleg set-up of his forebears. Behind the stillhouse's clapboard exterior is a state-of-the-art operation, with a diminutive copper pot still and a crack team to run it.

Taking around 11 days to complete the journey from muddy root vegetable to bottled spirit, the distillery's process is a slick one. For every bottle it wants to produce, 15lb (7kg) of potatoes are made into a thick potato soup (seasoned only with a little yeast) to create a fermentable broth. This low wine (which ends up at around 8% proof) is then distilled three times in a copper pot still, with each cut of spirit becoming purer and higher in alcohol than the last. The resulting spirit doesn't need to be filtered, and is simply cut with water from the Cold River aquifer that feeds the distillery before being bottled.

The slick packaging proudly proclaims Cold River Vodka as "a taste of Maine." While, arguably, Maine might prefer to be famous for its lobster rolls and Moxie carbonated drink than crisp liquor, you get the point—it's delicious. A clear example of what the field-to-glass process can produce.

Tasting notes: A big mouthfeel and characteristic potato sweetness dominate this smooth vodka. There's flavor there, undoubtedly, but this is a crowd-pleaser. Most likely the triple-distillation keeps any extreme notes at bay: a thoroughly likeable spirit that is excellent in martinis.
Price: $$$$
Other products: Cold River Blueberry Vodka; Cold River Gin
Web: coldrivervodka.com

Silver Tree American Small Batch Vodka (40% abv)

LEOPOLD BROS., DENVER, USA

Todd Leopold might just be the ginger-bearded, mild-mannered, publicity-shy face of true craft distilling. Along with his brother Scott ("who holds the pocket book and is the reason we're still in business"), Todd founded the Colorado-based distillery back in 1999 after a formal training in distilling in the USA and an informal training in brewing throughout Germany. Despite being one of the most awarded and successful craft distilleries in the States, Leopold Bros. remains resolutely small-scale, with only a couple of stills and a handful of employees. The number of spirits in the portfolio, however, is constantly on the rise (Todd's Willy Wonka-esque fascination with distilling ensuring that new projects are always bubbling away in the pipeline).

From Leopold's Gin, for which each botanical is individually distilled ("to ensure we hit its sweet spot," insists Todd) through to the various fruit liqueurs that are produced, Todd treats every product like it's his personal favorite, talking about each like a pet project. This is equally true when it comes to the vodka: "So, for us, it's potatoes and malted wheat that we use—

basically what you'd use for a Hefeweizen, one of those ideas left over from my German brewing days. We're trying to balance the spiciness you get from the wheat with the nice mouthfeel from the potato. Each component has a separate fermentation and separate distillation, and we also use barley so that we can break down all the starches, so there are no artificial enzymes. What we're aiming for is a nice, clean spirit."

The vodka is distilled seven times in tiny batches (the still is small enough to bear hug) and, unsurprisingly, needs no filtration prior to bottling. Each batch is named and numbered, giving a sense of the scale and craft that goes into every bottle.

Tasting notes: A whiff of spiciness on the nose from the grain, with black pepper at the fore; on the palate, this softens into a sweet, mouth-filling spirit with licorice notes.
Price: $$$
Other products: Leopold's Gin; a range of fruit liqueurs; Three Pins Alpine Herbal Liqueur; American Small Batch Whiskey; a range of fruit whiskeys; Absinthe Verte
Web: leopoldbros.com

Grand Teton Potato Vodka (40% ABV) TETON DISTILLERY, IDAHO, USA

Not only is the Grand Teton Distillery, founded by Bill and Lea Beckett in 2011, at the vanguard of exceptional vodka-making, it is also doing a good job evangelizing about the craft movement and spreading the word through its distilling masterclasses. That, of course, is one of the benefits of success: having garnered so many gold-standard accolades from the industry that you can practically hear the gong-cabinet clanking, other start-up distillers are keen to learn from these (relative) old-timers.

Bill and Lea built the distillery from the ground up. It was in a good position from the start, not only being located in one of the world's most scenic spots in the foothills of the Teton Mountains, but also because of the raw ingredients on its doorstep. The water comes from mountain snowmelt and its location slap-bang in the middle of America's potato state, Idaho, means local Russet spuds are to hand (there's even a potato

museum nearby!). Bill and Lea, along with master distiller John Boczar, control the whole production process, which begins with cooking huge vats of mashed potato. The potato beer is then distilled before going on to the 32-ft (10-m) high rectifying columns. The vodka is freeze filtered ("it works best when it's ice cold," says Lea) through charcoal and garnet to remove any off-notes, before being bottled.

Tasting notes: Lighter in body than some potato vodkas, this is nonetheless a pleasing combination of sweetness and spice, as well as a hint of pastry—tarte tatin, even, with imagination at full stretch.
Price: $
Other products: Vishnovka Russian Style Cherry Vodka; Blended American Whiskey Teton Moonshine; Spiced Apple Pie Flavored Whiskey Teton Moonshine
Web: tetondistillery.com

Black Cow Gold Top Vodka (40% abv)

BLACK COW DISTILLERY, DORSET, UK

Those who know Britain's West Country—with its bucolic vistas of lush, rolling hills and winding lanes—might be surprised to learn that the scene behind the five-bar gates of Childhay Manor Farm are more inspired by Tuva, a diminutive country in Siberia, than they are by Dorset's more traditional clotted cream and cheese-making practices. Here, dairy farmer Jason Barber and his business partner, Paul Archard, have translated the Siberian idea of turning yak's milk into vodka to their own herd of Holstein Friesian cows to produce a spirit that's artisan and unique to this part of the world.

The spirit-making process starts with the dawn milking, after which lush full cream from the grass-fed cows is taken off to be separated into curds and whey. The curds are used to make cheese—a rather delicious vintage Cheddar called Barber's 1833, should you ever come across it—and the whey, the thin, lactose- (milk sugar) and protein-filled liquid, is fermented into a milk beer with the aid of a lovingly cultivated yeast.

This low-alcohol liquid is then distilled and filtered in a process that Jason and Archie would rather keep shrouded in mystery, before being cut and packaged for the local market in its unusually slim-necked bottle. A number of celebrated British chefs, including Mark Hix and Hugh Fearnley-Whittingstall, have already championed the vodka, and there has been growing demand for new flavors or varieties to be added to the range. The plan for the moment, however, is to focus on top-quality milk vodka, and leave customers to make their own infusions at home. As it is, Black Cow is certainly proving a good way to get a few more pence per pint of milk for these farmers.

Great Britain Vodka Distilleries

• Chase   Adnams •

• Black Cow

Tasting notes: One rather expects a milk vodka to be cloudy, or at least especially suited to making White Russians, but this is a clear, fine sipping vodka with a sweetness and smoothness that really comes to the fore, along with a mineral note that's like wet stone. There's a whiff of milky creaminess, too—though it's hard to know whether that's the work of an overactive imagination.
Price: $$$
Other products: None currently
Web: blackcow.co.uk

Chase Original Potato Vodka (40% ABV)

CHASE DISTILLERY, HEREFORDSHIRE, UK

Doing what few craft distillers are able, though most aspire to, farmer William Chase—whose family business was based on growing potatoes and turning them into those delicious and posh "gourmet potato chips"—is one of the few artisan, independent producers who actually digs something out of the ground at one end of the production process and pours it into a bottle at the other.

Having been on a trip through the USA to look for chip-packing technology, Will came across a small, but brilliant, spud distillery. Duly inspired, he returned home with the idea and, in 2008, the first drops of unfiltered vodka ran off the still.

Once the King Edward and Lady Claire potatoes, which are grown on Will's Herefordshire farm, are gently harvested ("Treat potatoes like eggs at all times," staff are reminded), it takes around two weeks to turn them from their tuber state into a smooth vodka. First the spuds are mashed with brewer's yeast and fermented to produce low-alcohol wine. This then goes into a copper pot still—created especially for Chase—where each batch is distilled four times. Then, to get the vodka up to a high enough strength, it is rectified twice more in the 70-ft (21-m) high rectification column. Before bottling, water, drawn from the farm, is used to cut the spirit down to a more palatable strength of 40%.

The award-winning vodka that results from this impressively craft process is delicious in its own right: it is also a fantastic base for the range of flavored vodkas and gins that Chase produces. This stuff is craft from start to finish.

Tasting notes: Deliciously clean and almost creamy, with a white-pepper/aniseed spike, and a full mouthfeel that is akin to the oiliness of Brazil and macadamia nuts, this is a sipping vodka that's easily enjoyed neat. Neutral and flavorless this most definitely isn't, and it's all the better for it. It was awarded San Francisco World Spirits Competition Best Vodka (2010).

Price: $$$$

Other products: Chase English Oak Smoked Vodka; Chase Marmalade Vodka; Chase Rhubarb Vodka; Naked Chase Apple Vodka; Williams Chase Elegant Gin; Williams Chase GB Extra Dry Gin; Williams Chase Seville Orange Gin; Chase Summer Fruit Cup

Web: williamschase.co.uk

Adnams Longshore Premium Vodka (48% abv)

ADNAMS COPPER HOUSE DISTILLERY, SUFFOLK, UK

Keen beer drinkers among you may have twigged that Adnams is a name more usually associated with the pursuit of frothy pints than high-strength liquors—and, in fact, the coastal brew house was established in Southwold way back in 1872. Rather antiquated rules, put in place by the UK's Inland Revenue, used to prohibit distilling spirits on the same site as a brewery due to differing rates of tax on the grains that went into the two different products. However, in 2008, Jonathan Adnams, the company's chairman, managed to get an exception made for the company and the Copper House Distillery was transformed from a pipe dream to reality.

"As a brewing engineer, I have always been fascinated by the world of distilling and clearly understood the synergies and advantages in brewing and distilling activities on one site," Adnams says. Once permission to distil was granted, a lengthy research process into equipment and processes ensued in an attempt to find the technology that was best suited to turning the brew house's fantastic beer into a superlative spirit.

The set-up that resulted is a combination of stills from world-leading German manufacturer CARL and an American-style "beer stripping rectifying column" more commonly found in bourbon production. The first stage of the process is left in the hands of the experienced brewing team with locally grown grains (a combination of wheat, barley, and oats for the vodka) being mashed up and fermented with the brewer's yeast to create a wash (beer) of around 7.0%.

The wash is then run through the stripping still to extract as much high-quality alcohol as possible (those nasties that tag along are ditched in rectification). The low wines are then pumped into the 220-gallon (1,000-liter) pot still where they are heated, before being forced onward through the two rectification columns. Plenty of the spirit run is discarded at this stage, with the purest heart going on to be diluted with water and run through the rectification process again. The spirit that eventually runs off is exceptionally pure and barely needs filtering (although, in pursuit of perfection, it is).

Before bottling, the vodka is chilled to 28°F (-2°C) and filtered through paper to get rid of any particles that might make the spirit cloudy. Adnams are quick to point out that no carbon is used—the spirit is so pure that aggressive filtration isn't required.

Tasting notes: The thinking is that each of the cereals fermented for this vodka brings something to the party: barley lends an element of sweetness, while the wheat and oats contribute a sense of depth, mouthfeel, and lovely creaminess. The surprising result is a spirit that, although cut to a punchy 48% proof, hints more at clotted-cream toffee and brioche than it does palate-searing strength or pepper and spice. This one is gold-award-winning for a reason.
Price: $$$
Other products: Adnams Copper House Barley Vodka; Adnams North Cove Vodka; Adnams Copper House Distilled Gin; Adnams First Rate Gin; Adnams Sloe Gin; Adnams Morello Cherry Liqueur; Adnams Triple Sec Orange Liqueur; Adnams Winter Spiced Liqueur; Adnams Spirit of Broadside; Adnams Triple Grain Whisky; Adnams Absinthe Rouge
Web: adnams.co.uk

Vestal Kaszebe Vodka, 2013 (40% ABV)

VESTAL VODKA, POLAND

Vestal Vodka sits at the nexus of craft and rock'n'roll: it's stocked in high-end bars and super-premium department stores; it has a glittering array of celebrity fans, a famous muso relation, and top chefs and critics alike rate it. But the spirit's roots are as mud-covered as the best of 'em, firmly grounded in Polish potatoes.

The vodka's germination was an unusual one: New Zealander John Borrell, a former *TIME* magazine war photographer, settled in Poland over two decades ago. While one of his sons, Johnny, went on to become a not-insignificant musician (he's the frontman for Razorlight), son William decided to join his father in the enterprise of making vodka. Their ambition as to create a spirit that would be seen as an antidote to the anodyne, commercially produced, post-Communist liquors; a craft product worthy of vodka's spiritual homeland.

The thinking behind it came partly from wine and partly from whiskey. "In wine there is this concept of terroir. The idea that the grapes take on the essence of the climate and the soil and so on, and that's translated into the juice and therefore the wine," says William. "That's the way we felt vodka should be, made as it was several hundred years ago."

In the fields, the Borrells felt that the local terroir was best translated into vodka via the medium of "first earlies" (potatoes that are so young they are yet to form a proper skin). "These are low in starch (which is bad for vodka production), but packed with flavor," says William. "Obviously you need starch to create the sugars, so we had to make up for the low levels with the quantity of potatoes used, but it's worth it for the flavor." It takes more than six tonnes of potato to make 1,000 bottles of spirit.

So slight is the window for first earlies that Vestal production only happens for a few weeks a year in late August and September. "We want the potatoes out of the ground and into the mash in under 48 hours," William says. From there on in, however, the emphasis shifts from speed to patience. The 16ft (5m) column still, complete with its 48 "bubble plates," is fired up (powered by damp, smouldering hay, no less), while single-varietals of potato are distilled. Once the cut's taken, the spirit then sits in stainless-steel tanks for a couple of months so that the more volatile alcohols can disperse.

"This part of the business model is more whiskey-based," says William. "We're looking to give the spirit time; we want our vodka to be the equivalent of single malt, which is why we distil different varieties of potato, and have vintage variation." Only the blended vodka that comes from a number of potatoes is filtered, once, through a charcoal cartridge. "It removes a huge amount of flavor, so it's not something we would want to do with the single varieties," says William. "The most they see is a sieve to remove any bits…"

The two single varieties (from Vineta and red-skinned Asterix) aren't made every year—in 2012 flooded fields meant that the quality just wasn't there—which means rarer back-vintages can change hands for thousands of dollars. Assuming harvest and production have gone to plan, the new year's edition

tends to hit the market in spring. Also worth watching out for are their wood-aging experiments. Here, things get rather Heath Robinson; the boys have used French oak barrels, bourbon and Japanese chips, and some home-charred cherry wood ("we just toasted it on the farm") to create a vanilla-rich, creamy, wood-and-cherry-imbued vodka.

Vestal

Polish Vodka Distilleries

Tasting notes: Initial aromas sit somewhere between butterscotch and beeswax on the nose, which lulls you into a sweet sense of security before the spikier, licorice and nettle on the palate. Smooth and mouth-filling, sippable, and well worth dissecting. If you get your hands on a back-vintage, these tend to become sweeter and smoother with age.

Price: $$$

Other products: Vestal Blended Potato Vodka; Vestal Pomorze; Elderberry Liqueur

Web: vestalvodka.com

Karlsson's Gold Vodka (40% abv) SPIRITS OF GOLD, CAPE BJÄRE, SWEDEN

A very brief time spent looking at the curriculum vitaes of the men behind this vodka indicates a background that's not remotely craft—not unless you can bend the definition to include one of the world's most famous brands, that is. Peter Ekelund, Hans Brindfors, and Olof Tranvik were the marketing and design trinity who, among other coups, secured the services of Andy Warhol to help illustrate and bring to market—yes, you've guessed it—Absolut Vodka.

This time around, however, the vodka in question is a totally different beast: not different in the sense that there is anything home-spun about the operation, you understand—production is state-of-the-art rather than garden shed, and there is undoubtedly a substantial bank-roll behind the operation. Instead, the vodka is resolutely small-scale, super-premium quality, and made from… new potatoes.

In Sweden, as in much of the world, tiny virgin potatoes are a highly coveted crop, prized for their seasonality and earthy, creamy flavor; highly anticipated after the dark Swedish winter, they can sell at auction for up to $150 per pound (£94 per 450g). Most of the potatoes used to make vodka, on the other hand, are usually rather unloved and inelegantly handled. Karlsson's Gold uses seven different varieties of virgin potato for its vodka, each prized for its distinctive character and grown on Cape Bjäre, a sandy, picturesque peninsula. Seventeen lb (8kg) of potatoes go into each bottle.

The potato harvest, and thus the vodka production, takes place from June to September. Börje Karlsson, another Absolut alumni and the master distiller who gave his name to the vodka, oversees the distillation process. A wash is created from each of the varieties of potato being used—for you spud fans, these are Solist, Gammel Svensk Röd, Princess, Sankta Thora, Hamlet, Marine, and Celine—and these are individually distilled once in a copper-lined column still. Once all seven spirits have been produced, Karlsson blends them and the spirit is bottled. It's entirely unfiltered: his aim is to retain flavor and "to make a vodka with taste," not strip it out.

Tasting notes: "Just drink it as it is. If you don't like it, don't drink it," says distiller Börje Karlsson—a rather un-marketing-department-friendly sentiment perhaps, but evidence that he firmly believes in the taste of Karlsson's flagship vodka. And, indeed, it does have a very unusual flavor: on the nose, expect notes that are distinctly earthy and vegetal (think forest floor in springtime rather than moldering gym kit). On the palate, there's sweetness, cream, and a pistachio, green nuttiness. The suggested serve is neat over ice with a twist of fresh black pepper.
Price: $$$
Other products: Karlsson's also produces batch vodkas specific to different vintages.
Web: karlssonsvodka.com

Spirit of Hven Organic Vodka (40% ABV)

SPIRIT OF HVEN BACKAFALLSBYN, ØRESUND, SWEDEN

A tiny pot distillery, possibly the world's smallest, set against the wild backdrop of the diminutive Swedish island of Øresund makes the Spirit of Hven distillery textbook craft. Good news, then, that the spirits it produces—gin, whiskey, and vodka—are unmistakably high quality. Not only that, but its white spirits bring something rather unusual to the table: wood aging.

Henrik and Anja Molin, two of the island's 300-odd residents, are the husband-and-wife team behind the Backafallsbyn distillery, founded in 2008, which currently produces a smorgasbord of spirits. Whiskey is a particular focus, which means that they have an array of wood in situ. Despite being set up initially to concentrate entirely on the darker liquors, their foray into vodka and gin produced some spectacularly successful results (the gin, famously, is the only one stocked by the world's best restaurant, Noma in Copenhagen).

Overseeing the process from grain to glass, Henrik and Anja source their organic wheat both from the island and a number of producers in Europe, before malting and fermenting in house. After the initial distillation, the vodka sits in American oak for between six and 24 months, thus developing the complexity of flavor and character one would associate with a whiskey. The spirit then undergoes its middle distillation in Hven's long-necked, copper pot still to remove impurities without stripping out the mellow flavors which have imbued themselves in the spirit. The cut taken from this distillation is then rested for a further few months before being distilled one last time and taken down to bottling strength. Compared with the wham-bam approach that many distillers take (where vodka can be made, bottled, and shipped inside of 24 hours), this is an eye-openingly artisan process. Is it worth it? Well, the results certainly make for unusual and distinctive sipping.

Tasting notes: On the nose, there's vanilla and a hay-like sweetness, as well as a camomile note (think evening walks in late-summer meadows). On the palate, this is a round, smooth, and buttery spirit with a fresh crunch of black pepper. It's fantastic sipping, though Henrik also recommends trying it, Swedish-style, in a post-dinner coffee, which definitely works too.

Price: $$$

Other products: Organic Gin; Organic Aqua Vitae; Organic Summer Spirit; Organic Winter Spirit; Merak, Dubhe, and Urania Single Malt Whiskies

Web: hven.com

Swedish Vodka Distilleries

Karlsson's •
• Hven

GIN

It's virtually impossible to be a fan of craft spirits without appreciating gin—after all, for excellent practical reasons, it is the jumping-off point for most start-up distillers who find it a financially viable and creatively exciting liquor with which to launch their enterprises (more on this momentarily). There is, too, a pleasing notion that a spirit which was once vilified and blamed for the rot of society—dubbed "mother's ruin" and propagandized by the likes of 18th-century satirist William Hogarth in his famous etching *Gin Lane*—has, having cleaned up its act as a result of commercial distilling, now cycled its way back toward its bathtub roots (albeit without the associated consequences of disintegrating moral standards).

A CORNERSTONE OF CRAFT DISTILLING

Assuming there is no need to preach to the converted on the merits of gin—to coax you from the safe ground of vodka or to reassure you that we are not about to slide into a new era of botanical-fueled vice, we can look instead at why gin is so crucial to the craft distiller. Firstly, it is unaged. This means that a start-up producer's initial financial investment can become lucrative more quickly: he doesn't have to invest any money in wooden barrels in which to mature the spirit, or a warehouse to store it in for a few decades, or to have his capital tied up in a product that won't be ready to sell for a number of years. Secondly, unlike vodka, there is more to gin than simply alcohol, water, and packaging: the recipe for botanicals to be included can be as outlandish or conventional as the producer's personality, giving a certain scope for creativity and flair.

Pride of place

There are also very few geographical regulations governing where gin can be produced (even "London" gin simply refers to a certain type of production process rather than a point of origin—more on that shortly). In fact, there are very few regulations at all concerning gin, other than the inclusion of juniper somewhere on the list of botanicals. And, last but not least (and perhaps rather surprisingly), gin producers don't actually need to make the base alcohol themselves—in fact, only a handful do. Instead, the producer will buy in a very high-percentage, totally neutral, grain alcohol, which they then distil with botanicals to transform it from mere ethanol into mighty gin.

What is a botanical?

This one's easy: a botanical is simply an ingredient used to flavor gin—much as, say, toffee or lemon could be used to flavor vodka. Theoretically, at least, you could use anything in your botanical mix—and as many pieces of flora as you fancy—as long as juniper is included, which it must be by law.

The reason for juniper's involvement is archaic, and comes from gin's precursor, genever (see pages 62–69), which is a Dutch spirit that became popular as it was exported by traders and soldiers from the 1500s onward. To make Genever, the juniper berry was originally distilled with malt wine in order to produce a spirit that was only intended to be medicinal. Bartenders undoubtedly have much to thank early physicians for.

The small, hard, almost black juniper berries grow in the wild, much like the sloe, and lend gin its characteristically aromatic flavors of pine and citrus, as well as a floral element that is akin to lavender. Juniper is spicy, too—in fact, the Romans used it as an alternative to rare and expensive black pepper.

Other commonly used—and rather fanciful-sounding—botanicals include angelica root, licorice, coriander seed, cardamom, cinnamon, and citrus peel. Angelica is a native of Scandinavia (where, apparently,

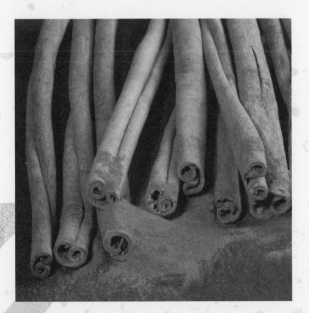

it was used to flavor reindeer milk), and northern Europe and Asia, where it has been used variously to defend against everything from colds to the plague and—ironically—even intoxication. In gin, it lends an "emulsifying" property, bringing together the other oils, as well as adding its own base, peppery, herbaceous notes. Licorice—and here we are talking about the plant and its root rather than something that comes from the Bassett's factory—is included for sweetness, warmth, and aniseed-type flavors. Coriander seed, cinnamon, and cardamom need little explanation (other than a trip to your spice rack if you've forgotten their exotic, fragrant aromas), while citrus peel is most commonly used in the form of lemons—especially the oil-rich, sweet, Italian varieties—or grapefruit. Recently, thanks to the growth in popularity of Hendrick's, cucumber has also earned its place in the botanical lexicon.

Craft distillers are bringing a more imaginative take to the list of botanicals, so expect to see a touch of the wild (literally) and wacky alongside this more conventional bunch. The process by which a alcohol is introduced to botanicals (steeping, steaming, macerating, and so on) is another way in which the distiller can control the intensity and style of his gin.

"OFFICIAL" STYLES OF GIN

London Dry

Think about any of the classic gins you're used to drinking, and chances are they're London Dry. This is one of the only styles of gin to be governed by rules: for example, it must be made from natural ingredients with no artificial additives (so, reassuringly, this means real botanicals rather than chemical flavoring); it must be distilled to at least 70% ABV; and it must be—as the name indicates—dry, so the amount of sugar that can be added is limited. But, despite the fact it's called "London" gin, it need not have anything to do with England's capital city; in fact, only a handful of gins are actually distilled there (though plenty of the stuff is drunk).

Old Tom

Poor Old Tom—once it was lauded on the cocktail scene and championed by backstreet drinkers, but it became almost obsolete in the 20th century, as its sweeter style fell out of favor with moralists and consumers alike. Legend has it that Old Tom got its name from a rather unusual dispensing method: vendors would hang a plaque of a tom cat in the street, customers would drop their coins into a slot, and in return a measure of gin would be dispensed from a tube under the cat's paws. Thanks, largely, to a generation of bartenders whose alcohol archaeology unearthed a number of recipes from the archive, which called for Old Tom, there has recently been something of a resurgence of the category.

Plymouth

Unlike misleading London Dry, Plymouth Gin—as its name suggests—does have to be distilled in Plymouth (that's Plymouth, Devon, not Massachusetts, USA), where its roots date back to 1793. Its PGI status is a somewhat limiting factor, however, and despite the best efforts of local naval recruits to support the area's endeavors, there remains only one Plymouth Gin (imaginatively called Plymouth Gin), which is sweeter and more aromatic than classic London Dry. It might not be a big category, but it still counts.

American

An emerging philosophy, as much as it is a style, the American Gin category is a relative newcomer (especially when you're comparing it with Old Tom…). These gins aren't bound by legal definitions, and craft distillers are a renegade bunch and are increasingly pushing the boundaries in terms of styles of gin. American Gins tend to be sweeter than London Dry gins and also less obviously juniper-led: the aim of the category is to allow other botanicals to come into play.

The craft gin pioneers

Like the cool older sibling whose records you wanted to listen to, whose clothes you wanted to wear, and whose friends you really wanted to hang out with, Sipsmith—the London-based distiller, which was at the vanguard of craft in the UK when it set up the operation in 2009—has inspired adulation and provided motivation for the small-scale distilling scene in Britain and beyond.

Sipsmith's success came not only from the creation of a couple of good base products (initially, these majored on a serious gin and vodka), but also because of canny timing and phenomenal marketing of the brand. In short, by securing a licence to run their still, Prudence, in their garage, Sam Galsworthy and Fairfax Hall unwittingly created a formula which would be the blueprint for countless craft imitators to come.

Sipsmith's gin and vodka have now flowed so far into the mainstream—internationally as well as at home—that its story needs little telling, but to recap: having set up their German CARL still, Prudence, and her sibling, Patience, in Hammersmith, London, Sam, Fairfax, and their distiller, Jared, set about buying a quality barley spirit to use as their base alcohol. To make their vodka, the boys set about re-distilling this barley base to the highest quality, adding not only copper-pot character to the spirit as it ran off the still, but also imbuing it with a narrative that could be told on the bottle. For the gin, this involved a one-shot distillation of the botanicals. (This means that, rather than creating a super-strong botanical concentrate which is then diluted—like cordial—with base alcohol, Sipsmith charges each and every distillation with the requisite amount of botanicals for that particular batch, which results in a much rounder, more integrated spirit.)

But this is not simply a success story based on quality; it is also one of personality. From the very first batch that was produced, gin and vodka bottles were individually numbered and a little story about "the day it was distilled" posted on the website (so, for example, batch number LDG/689 July 23, 2014 was made on "Gin & Sausages Day" because the "Smiths were serving G&Ts at a gin-and-sausage-themed art installation—those crazy cats!). This storytelling—from the top-level branding down to the batch-by-batch micro-scale—is critical to their success: when you drink Sipsmith, you're not just tasting a small-batch spirit, you're also soaking up the carefully crafted narrative and personality that surrounds it. This is what set Sipsmith leagues ahead of other distillers in the UK, and powered their stratospheric success.

But what of those distillers who have followed where Sipsmith led? While some haven't quite lived up to the mark, others have (arguably) matched what Sam, Fairfax, and Jared are doing—and, when looking for disciples who have the skill, set-up, and philosophy sorted, the gold-award-winning Warner Edwards distillery (see pages 54–55) is a very good place to start. Then there are the people like Sacred (see page 56), who aren't afraid to do things differently —as the below photograph of their home set-up shows. It is this diversity that makes this such an exciting time for gin lovers everywhere.

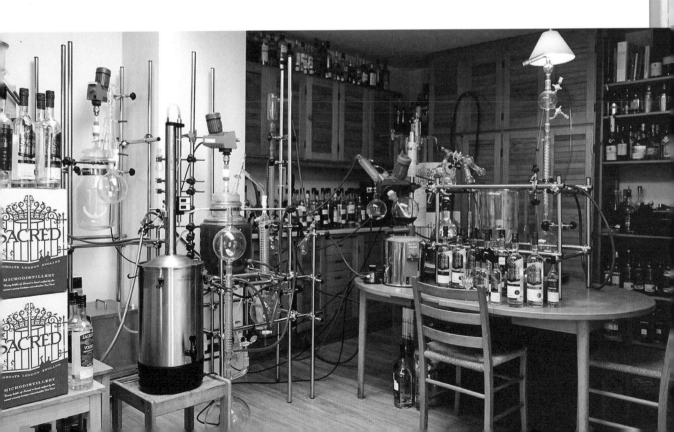

Harrington Dry Gin

(40% abv)

WARNER EDWARDS, HEREFORDSHIRE, UK

"Don't wait for your ship to come in—go out and meet it," says Tom Warner, one half of this brilliant British distilling partnership, who, along with fellow distiller Sion Edwards, has unquestionably done just that. In a few short years, the pair has gone from back-of-cigarette-packet business plans to a barn-based distillery producing a gin that has racked up double-gold trophies at the San Francisco World Spirits Competition.

Sion and Tom both come from farming families, and first met at agricultural college in 1997. As with many bonds formed in halls of residence and campus housing, that early friendship—rooted in a shared love of numerous important things such as a pint—proved to be strong and, on graduating, the pair (via a spell in the real world) elected to go into business together. "We bounced round a lot of ideas and did cigarette-packet feasibility studies, which ranged from putting in anaerobic digesters through to growing floral crops and distilling essential oils," says Tom. "Then it dawned on us that when the flowers weren't in season, you would use the still to make alcohol for the rest of the year—and that really sparked our interest.

"We started tuning in to the market—the more we read and the more we researched, the more excited we got. Although, initially, we started by looking at producing vodka in North Wales on Sion's family farm, over the course of four years' planning and business research we migrated to gin: gin was our spirit (not in a very sophisticated kind of way—we were more 10 pints and move on to G&Ts—but that's how it began). Now, we are all about the martinis…"

The boys' farming background meant that they wanted to start by growing the grain they would later distil. "That was the dream, but we soon realized that the costs involved were absolutely astronomical—prohibitive." Their pockets not being deep enough, Sion and Tom looked to the gin world, to Tom's farm in Herefordshire, and to the common practice of using a bought-in, neutral grain spirit. "We found out that almost all gin distilleries buy this in—it's the industry standard, partly because you're not actually allowed to make the alcohol for gin in the same pot as the gin itself, so it wouldn't really affect our provenance… Then again, we still want to grow our own barley one day…" (There are also plans for a whiskey.)

Buying in base spirit also gave Warner Edwards an advantage when it came to dealing with UK Revenue and Customs, a body that can prove famously troublesome for some start-up distilleries. "The Revenue doesn't give out licences for more than you need: although we applied for the full distiller's licence, actually we were awarded a rectifier's licence on the basis that—initially at least—rectification is what we needed to do. Now we've done our probationary year, we've been able to add a couple of things on to the licence, such as maceration so that we can soak fruit or sloe berries with alcohol. Every time we've added a new product with a new raw material and a new process, we have to notify HMRC and have that added on to our licence as an appendix."

Other than making their operation legal, the most significant obstacles were raising the capital for, and selecting the specifications of, their stills. "When we placed the order for Curiosity we were doing our diligence on stills: at that point, the two big guys who had started were Chase and Sipsmith and they had both gone with CARL as their still manufacturer—in fact, just about every craft distiller in the UK went CARL, unless they were using an alembic still. We were the first small guys to do something different—for us, it was a question of better build quality. Ours really is the Rolls Royce of stills from Arnold Holstein: it does a tremendous job—especially as it has a patented catalyzer on the top, which increases the copper surface area, helping to produce a very clean spirit. Since we've started, they've had orders for 10 stills in the UK now (I reckon we've done a very good advertizing job for them!)"

With the still in place and the big strategic decisions made about the alcohol they were going to produce, Tom and Sion had one other major decision to make: "Water," says Tom. "It's a key element, and we were lucky enough to be able to source it from the farm where we have our own natural springs (there are seven in the top two fields). In fact, the village is said to be built on rock and water, and it's exceptionally good. So, Sion and I drove round on a quad together (it was all a bit *Brokeback Mountain*)—we drank out of all the different springs and decided which one was best just on the taste/flavor profile and that was it."

Great British Gin Distilleries

Warner Edwards •
Sacred •

Tom and Sion, having started out with a great idea, but a limited amount of experience, have got deeper and deeper into the craft gin world. "Now we're the old boys on the block—we've been distilling for 18 months and we feel like the forefathers. It is crazy the number of new distilleries opening up—and we think it's great—and we're really on the soapbox with regards to what craft should be.

"The big guys—those with the multi-million-pound marketing budgets—they're the competition. But the craft guys, we are all the same selling force talking about a different way of producing, and I don't just mean different botanicals: we are more flexible in what we can do and we are really the exciting end of the market. We can throw ideas at the wall and see what sticks in terms of product development, whereas the large distilling companies have to spend several years and several million pounds launching a product that might not work in the end. The reality is, we can try something different tomorrow if we want to."

"The key thing about craft distilling," weighs in Sion, "is that it is supposed to be artisanal. It doesn't have to be bonkers—instead, it just needs to be top quality. For us, as it turns out, this means that everything we do is probably the hardest way of doing it… With the bottles, this means that we hand-wrap the copper wire round the neck of every bottle; we wax-dip each one, we put the ribbon round each one, and we hand-apply all the labels. With the still, it means that we oversee every run, we do a one-shot distillation, which, although it's very inefficient, gives us the best results when it comes to gin. And, even though it costs more to do it, we run the still very slowly to make sure that the gin is exceptionally smooth. It adds up, and it makes for a great product…"

Tasting notes: "There is slight batch-to-batch variation with our gin," says Sion. "But anyone who's worried about that should be told to shut up—that's craft distilling. We are not homogenized, standardized rubbish; there's no guy in a lab coat adding fusel oils to create certain flavors. There will be variation, but that's why every batch is numbered and every bottle is numbered. Yes, batches are different—but they'll all be good, they'll all be smooth, and they'll all be packed with botanical flavor." And, which flavors are they exactly? Well, the barley-based spirit is infused with—among other things—elderflower grown on the farm, which gives the gin an inherently floral, mouthwatering elegance that sits alongside citrus (lemon) peel and candied-ginger sweetness and warmth. The juniper-based pine provides structure throughout the mouthful, ensuring it remains big, bold, and smooth. Sensational.
Price: $$$
Other products: Elderflower Infused Gin; Sloe Gin; Victoria's Rhubarb Gin
Web: warneredwards.com

Sacred Gin (40% abv)

SACRED SPIRITS COMPANY, LONDON, UK

Ian Hart's tale of credit-crunch-based disenfranchisement with the financial sector and his search for a career with more soul is not an uncommon one. The path that led him to start vacuum distilling the different botanicals for gin in his own home is perhaps less usual: "I bought an old RAF oscilloscope on eBay and started trying to invent things—laser systems, semiconductor Tesla coils, microwave radar systems, and so on," he explains.

Thankfully for gin drinkers, most of Ian's inventions were dead-ends, but somewhere in this mad-scientist questing, Ian discovered his spirit-based calling. "Every Sunday evening, we would go to our local pub, where some of the regulars and the bar staff would taste our most recent recipe. One night, everyone unanimously declared that our 23rd recipe was a great gin—and importantly—unlike other London Dry Gins. The landlord Martin Harley said that if we bottled it, he would put it behind the bar. That gave us the impetus to bottle our first 2,500 bottles. It became known as Sacred Gin because one of our botanicals is frankincense, AKA Boswellia sacra—hence Sacred."

Ian's approach to distilling, you may have guessed, is also less than conventional (there are no gleaming pot stills in his set-up). In fact, his innovative nexus of pipes and tubes and jars and so on, is spun—like a spider's web—in his north London home. Here, Ian receives the base alcohol ("Very few gin distilleries in the UK produce their own alcohol," he says) and begins the process of infusing the botanicals. "We use glassware and extremely high-quality English wheat spirit, which has been re-distilled many thousands of times (in an extremely high-tech modern still in Manchester) for extra purity, and organic fresh botanicals. This, combined with a low temperature, creates an exact distillation of nature's true aromas, without any damage or change to the botanicals associated with hotter stills." His process gives Sacred a big advantage over his pot-still-using brethren, argues Ian: "Think of the smell of fresh torn basil leaves compared to cooked basil, or the difference between fresh-cut oranges rather than cooked (i.e. marmalade). So, our distillates are extraordinarily fresh and pure in comparison with those made by copper pot stills."

In layman's terms, Sacred's process can be described pretty simply. All its carefully selected, fresh (never dried) organic botanicals are macerated separately for four to six weeks in high-quality English grain spirit at 50% ABV. This discrete maceration ensures that each botanical retains its own distinctive character. "This is a seriously long maceration period—most distilleries are content to macerate overnight," says Ian. Then, once the flavors have been fully infused into the spirit, the strained botanical liquors are distilled separately under glassware using vacuum distillation: "This means that, instead of a traditional pot still, each macerated botanical liquor is poured into a glass flask and a vacuum pump pulls air and vapors out of the container, reducing air pressure and thus the liquid's boiling point. The higher the vacuum, the colder the temperature at which alcohol and aromatics can be distilled." The resulting individual distillates are then blended to create Sacred Gin. And it really does taste quite extraordinary. Trying Sacred is one of those experiences that shifts one's gin compass a few degrees toward finding the spirit's true north. It is a wonderfully clean, crisp, and pure product: an idiosyncratic ambition brilliantly realized.

Tasting notes: This double gold-medal winner, now exported worldwide, is certainly one to include in your gin armory. Citrus dances zestily across the palate, twinned with a live wire of pine and juniper (crushed pine needles) and an extraordinary, delicate, warming spice that lingers in complex and nuanced layers. For those who are interested in exploring how different botanicals manifest themselves and combine, Sacred sells them individually, too, so you can blend your own gin should you wish, or simply soak up the essence of the separate flavors.

Price: $$$

Other products: Sacred Cardamom Gin; Sacred Christmas Pudding Gin; Sacred Coriander Gin; Sacred Licorice Gin; Sacred Orris Gin; Sacred Pink Grapefruit Gin; Sacred London Dry Vodka; Sacred Organic Vodka; Sacred Spiced English Vermouth; and Sacred Rosehip Cup

Web: sacredspiritscompany.com

Swedish Gin Distilleries

Hernö •

Hernö Gin (40.5% ABV)

HERNÖ, ÅNGERMANLAND, SWEDEN

It all started on Tuesday, May 29, 2012, when Kierstin arrived at the distillery: with her unique curves and polished presentation, Jon Hillgren was in love. His handmade copper still, which was to be the beating heart of his new distillery, was perfect.

Duly ensconced in the red-walled, "summer-hut-styled" cabin-in-the-woods (above), it was a few short months before Kierstin was being fired up in anger to produce the first runs of Hernö Gin. Jon had curated a recipe based on the gins that he loved during his time in the UK bar trade, also bringing a native touch of Sweden to the mix.

Created in a one-shot distillation, he first introduced Hungarian-sourced juniper and Bulgarian coriander to the warmed, wheat-based spirit: this power couple were then left to infuse for a day (a potent head-start on the other botanicals) in the belly of the 55-gallon (250-liter) CARL still. Then, the remaining ingredients, which, alongside the usual citrus suspects, include decidedly Swedish lingon berries and unusually British meadowsweet, are brought into the distillation. The final cut is diluted only with well water before being bottled.

Tasting notes: Tasted alongside any American-style gin, this seems startlingly pine- and juniper-led, with a crushed-pine-needle freshness and an exotic confusion of citrus and spice. There's a Moroccan orange cake sweetness and buttery complexity to finish.
Price: $$$
Other products: Hernö Juniper Cask Gin; Hernö Navy Strength Gin
Web: hernogin.com

In spite of being a relative newcomer, Hernö's classic gin has already garnered the industry's most desirable gin accolades. Meanwhile, its more potent siblings—the Navy Strength and the Juniper Cask—point to more exciting things to come.

Ransom Old Tom Gin (44% abv)

RANSOM SPIRITS, OREGON, USA

Tad Seestedt's knowingly named enterprise makes little secret of the fact that it took a fistful of credit cards and a substantial amount more determination to coax his winery-come-craft-distillery into being, but in 1997 his dream became a reality. The business was initially focused on boutique wine, but a decade after its inception, the craft spirit movement provided the requisite inspiration for a distilling arm.

Set against the backdrop of high-quality viticulture, Tad was never going to shirk the grain-to-glass mentality and, indeed, his distilling arm is rooted in good agriculture. He grows his own barley on the farm, or where the mash bill dictates other requirements, and sources locally grown organic grains. These are brought into the distillery to be milled, mashed, and fermented on a weekly cycle, before they meet their destiny: Ransom's Gallic old-fashioned pot still.

Without computers monitoring the spirit run or assessing the cut, the distiller's nose is the most important piece of kit in the distillery—Tad makes his cuts by taste and smell alone. The heart of the heart—the smallest and purest part of the run—is reserved for Ransom's phenomenal (and multi-gold-award-winning) Old Tom Gin, the recipe for which can be attributed to the gray cells of cocktail historian David Wondrich. The base spirit comes from malted barley, which is combined with a botanical-infused corn spirit (actually quite a conventional gin-mix that includes juniper, orange peel, lemon peel, cardamom, coriander seeds, and angelica root). These are blended and then re-distilled together to create a malty, herbal, smooth, and satisfying whole that's then cask-rested in French oak for a number of months.

Tasting notes: Orange oil and a crushed pine-needle intensity on the nose; on the palate, more of the same, but with a dry and mouthwatering impression of bitters. Moreish.
Price: $$$$
Other products: Ransom Dry Gin; Small's Gin; Gewürztraminer Grappa; The Vodka; Henry DuYore's Straight Bourbon Whiskey; The Emerald 1865 Straight American Whiskey; WhipperSnapper Oregon Spirit Whiskey
Web: ransomspirits.com (see also *Vermouth*, page 149)

US Gin Distilleries

• House Spirits
Ransom

• St George

Smooth Ambler •

Aviation Batch Distilled American Gin (42% abv)

HOUSE SPIRITS DISTILLERY, OREGON, USA

"One of the generally agreed points about craft distilling is that it is a successor to the craft beer brewing revolution," says Tom Mooney, co-owner and CEO of House Spirits. "A lot of the people who were involved in beer came across to spirits—and we were no different." So it was that, spearheaded by founder Christian Krogstad, the distillery came into being over a decade ago. "We have also been closely associated with the cocktail renaissance and have gone out of our way to be knowledgeable and relevant to the cocktail world," Tom goes on, alluding to the final member of the partnership: former bartender Ryan Magarian. "We tend to see our products as tools for other people to work with and not as the final products."

It was this synergy between the bar trade and booze manufacture that brought Aviation into being. Christian was a man with a distillery; Ryan was a man with a dream for a new kind of gin. "Ryan had a vision for a new expression of gin that was better-suited to contemporary palates than classic gin," Tom explains. "Christian had been experimenting with gin without seeing a specific need in the market to address (for him it was more, "Hey, I have a still, I like gin... let's see what comes out"). Once they started working together, over the course of about a year and several dozen batches, they created a gin that is now distributed around the USA, around the world, and is one of the highest-rated gins you can buy." No mean feat.

Ryan's concept for the gin didn't entirely dispense with tradition—he researched the flavors that would have been typical a hundred years ago when gin cocktails were big business—but wanted a botanical blend that moved the juniper down a few notches and let other flavors into the party. He was certainly taking a risk—"It was a gamble that a large company wouldn't necessarily have taken," says Tom. To make the spirit, a bought-in, neutral-grain spirit is gently infused with the botanicals, including more unusual specimens such as lavender and sarsaparilla. Rather than a copper pot, Aviation is distilled in a 400-gallon (1,800-liter), stainless-steel still before being reduced down to bottling strength and packaged up on site.

Tasting notes: A gin for those who like their spirit smooth and floral, rather than dry and fresh, the nose is a delicate balance of lavender and juniper. The mouthfeel is remarkable: rich and oily, giving an impression of immense smoothness, but kept on its toes with citrus and spice. The finish lingers pleasantly.
Price: $$$
Other products: Krogstad Festlig Aquavit; Krogstad Gamle Aquavit; House Spirits Series Liqueurs; Volstead Vodka; Westward Oregon Straight Malt Whiskey
Web: housespirits.com (see also page 10)

"As a company, we are so similar to what craft distilling is as a whole," says Tom. "House Spirits is a bunch of people who really understand their craft, who are at the top of their game, who are making great things that are different enough that no one else would take the risk. And then we work way too hard to make them a success."

Terroir Gin (45% abv)

ST. GEORGE SPIRITS, CALIFORNIA, USA

With more than 30 years of craft production under its belt, this elder statesman of US distilling deserves more than just a respectful tip of the hat. "When Jörg [Rupf] founded St. George Spirits in 1982, he laid the groundwork for the modern American artisan distillation movement," states the company's website—a claim that's far from marketing puff. From its inception as a one-still, eau-de-vie enterprise to its current larger-scale incarnation, St. George has retained a freewheeling, infectious creativity that's the envy of the industry.

In spirits circles, at least, the story of St. George is well known—after all, it's provided a blueprint for legions of distillers to follow. German-born Jörg, a qualified lawyer by profession, was lured to the sunshine-soaked climes of the States on a sabbatical. However, it wasn't the constitutional law that captured his imagination, but rather San Francisco Bay's lush abundance of gorgeous fruit: his Black Forester's instinct for distilling was awakened.

Busily batch-producing his spirits in the early Eighties, Jörg was a lone figure on the small-scale distilling scene. His trailblazing antics attracted others, however, and he soon began training a number of fellow enthusiasts (all of whom have gone on to set up key distilleries—Clear Creek, for example—in their own right). Jörg, a perfectionist by nature, quested constantly to improve his *eau-de-vies*. In the mid-Nineties, around the same time as nuclear-scientist-turned-brewer Lance Winters arrived on the scene, St. George began to dabble in whiskey distillation. Lance, with a hunger to distil which equalled that of Jörg's, stuck around: today, he's the quirky, outlandish, and wilfully creative Master Distiller behind some of the most brilliant spirits St. George produces.

The distillery's Terroir Gin is a case in point. Lance has an almost feverish desire to capture the essence of the local landscapes—parks and bays—in his spirits. Terroir Gin is a handsome attempt to do just this. While some components are distilled in isolation (the fir and sage are cooked up in the 55-gallon (250-liter) still, others are gently infused via a botanicals basket or go directly into the larger pot still. There is method in this particular madness: the different preparation methods iron out seasonal variations in the ingredients and allow for a meticulous blend. Measuring the success of this tribute to the Golden State requires you to have visited this neck of the woods, but as for its success as a gin? That's beyond doubt.

Tasting notes: Pine, pine, pine on the nose—like being in a car with a Christmas tree. On the palate, this festive assault gives way to lovely, bay-leaf, summertime warmth and citrus.
Price: $$$
Other products: Botanivore Gin; Dry Rye Gin; Fruit Brandies, Fruit Liqueurs, and a Coffee Liqueur; St. George California Agricole Rum; B&E Bourbon; Single Malt Whiskey; Absinthe Verte (see also *Absinthe*, page 145)
Web: stgeorgespirits.com

Smooth Ambler Greenbrier Gin (40% abv)

SMOOTH AMBLER, WEST VIRGINIA, USA

We've all read something, or met someone, or been somewhere and thought: "I could do that; I'd love to do that," but there aren't many of us who convert that thought into action. Having been inspired by an article on craft distilling in *TIME* magazine, son and father-in-law John Little and Tag Galyean went beyond mere bar-room philosophizing about how much they'd like to start a distillery and actually did it. Together, they have created the gloriously grain-to-glass set-up that is Smooth Ambler.

There's an easy, appealing, "good-things-come-to-those-who-wait" philosophy surrounding the Appalachian-based distillery, where the excitement generated by what they're doing is counterpointed with a sense of confidence that there is no need to rush their products to market. (For example, they've released a series of independent bottlings to keep the coffers full while their whiskies come to fruition.) The small team on the distillery floor—usually three guys—oversees the arrival of the corn from a local farmer (they buy everything he can produce) and grain; then the milling, mashing, fermentation, and aging.

Their Swiss Army knife of a still is a work of hybrid beauty: it's a copper pot still when required, but also has a column-still capability, which can be pulled into play when lighter spirits are being produced. While Smooth Ambler's whiskey range is quietly growing, John and Tag have also created a couple of sensational white spirits: SA's grain-based Whitewater Vodka, which is triple-distilled from a mash bill of 68 percent corn with the remainder being an even split of malted wheat and barley, forms the high-quality basis of the Greenbrier Gin and Barrel-Aged Gin. (The latter sits in bourbon barrels for three months, gaining both color and complexity.) Greenbrier sits firmly in the emerging "American-style Gin" category that puts juniper on the back seat and allows other interesting botanicals to the fore.

Tasting notes: A citrus fragrance on the nose, along with a distinct crunch of pepper, makes this an inviting drop. To taste, there's an almost oily, silky mouthfeel and sense of sweet spice.
Price: $$$$
Other products: Stillhouse Collection Barrel-Aged Gin; Whitewater Vodka; Yearling Bourbon Whiskey; and a number of independent bottlings that appear under the "Old Scout" label
Web: smoothambler.com

GENEVER

Genever (aka jenever, or old Dutch gin) has been the national liquor of the Netherlands and Belgium for some 500-plus years—more if you count its use as a medicinal tonic. But it only truly began to seep back into the bartender's lexicon around a decade ago, when demand for the old styles of alcohol which had been used in vintage recipes began to grow, and brands such as Bols launched a genever, so feeding enthusiasm in the market.

A DUTCH CLASSIC

The resurgence of interest was not before time: for several hundred years, this malt-based, juniper-infused spirit had been consigned to a mere footnote in the history of gin (the precursor to "mother's ruin," Old Tom, and London Dry). As for its significance in whiskey's past, genever barely gets a mention, probably unfairly. Single-malt specialist Dave Broom argued recently in *Whisky Magazine* that "bar some quirk of fate, there's every possibility you would be reading *Jenever Mag* and not *Whisky Mag* and that whiskey as we know it might only exist as a weird Jenever variation rather than the other way round."

To put the spirit in the context of its 15th-century beginnings, one has to look back to a time when Christopher Columbus was still navigating the globe and before Europe had even discovered the potato. At around this time, the first recorded recipe to use juniper in a potable beverage was committed to manuscript by a Dutch merchant. The document is lauded by gin lovers, in particular, as the first evidence of juniper being employed in a non-medicinal context, even though, in this instance, it was being made with grape-based wine rather than a grain spirit. (A team led by cocktail historian and writer David Wondrich is currently trying to recreate and bring to market this original recipe, named 1495 Gin.)

If we trust, then, that the spirit's beginnings were around 1495, give or take, one need only fast-forward a few years until the first texts record grain-distillate being used—a trend fueled by the fact that Holland was at war with the wine-producing French. In 1575, the Bols distillery, the oldest remaining operation, and undoubtedly the most famous producer, was founded and, around a hundred years later, the first use of the word genever was recorded. The spirit, as we still know it today, was taking shape, characterized by a blend of malt wine (distilled from a combination of rye, wheat, maize, and malted barley) and a neutral grain spirit that was distilled with an often potent combination of botanicals.

Beyond Holland

Genever became not just locally popular: with trading routes spanning the globe, the spirit followed Dutchmen's explorations—notably when the Dutch East India Company was formed in the first years of the 17th century—and it was taken to England when William of Orange ascended the throne in 1689. The traders were also bringing back new and exotic spices which could be used in the botanical blend. As a result, demand for genever grew exponentially and production gradually became more and more concentrated in the town of Schiedam (below), where the herring fishery industry gave way to the influx of distillers, who came not only from across the Netherlands and Belgium, but also from Germany.

The genever industry continued to boom throughout the 18th century, with grain being imported by boat where Holland could not meet with demand. Production reached its peak in the mid-19th century, with more than 400 distilleries in operation and thousands of Schiedammers thus employed. Jobs varied, from the men who stoked the pot stills with coal to the millers who operated the 20-plus giant windmills that towered above the city. Five of these remain today, including *Da Walvisch* ("The Whale") and *De Vrijheid* ("The Freedom"). Furnishing the needs of the distilleries were teams of porters, who ran goods all over Schiedam—when hands were needed, the porter's lodge would ring a bell, those in need of work had seven minutes to run to the building where they rolled a dice; the man with the highest roll got the work.

Though Schiedam is no longer the center for production that it once was, genever has become a European Union regulated product—governed by an AOC status, which means it can now only be produced in the Netherlands or Belgium*, its historic home, where it must adhere to certain rules depending on the style of genever being produced.

This is true of the classic styles outlined on page 64; a few exceptions exist and so technically there are 11 AOC areas, some of which are in France and Germany.

THE TRIO OF GENEVER STYLES

There are three main types of genever: *Oude*, *Jonge*, and *Korenwijn*. Although the difference between the first two sounds like a product of age, it's actually a chronological one: *Oude* ("old") having been invented before *Jonge* ("young"). The rules governing them are as follows:

Oude

This must be made from at least 15 percent *moutwijn* ("malt wine"), which is the rye, corn, wheat, and barley pot-distilled spirit that is combined with a gin-like, botanical-infused, neutral spirit. It may contain no more than ¾oz (20g) of sugar per 34 fl oz (1 liter). Oude-style genevers are occasionally barrel-aged prior to bottling, though this is not a prerequisite for the style, which is naturally malty and flavorful. If you see the term *Graanjenever* on a label, this refers to the fact that its contents are made from 100 percent grain-based spirit (*graan* meaning "grain," rather than great, which it's often mistaken for!).

Jonge

A relatively modern style, Jonge genever was conceived as recently as the Fifties. This new variation was introduced in response to an ebbing demand for the traditional, botanical-dominated, and malt-laden style, which also coincided with higher quality neutral spirits becoming more easily available. Regulations state Jonge genever need only contain around five percent malt wine, and cannot contain more than 15 percent, along with a permitted ⅓oz (10g) of sugar per 34 fl oz (1 liter) maximum.

Korenwijn

This translates as "corn wine," and is perhaps less common than the other styles of genever. This malt-dominated style must contain at least 51 percent malt wine, along with a maximum sugar level of ¾oz (20g). If it is aged, which is not a requirement, then this must take place in wood barrels for at least a year.

Craft genever producers

Genever production has not been rocked in the same way as more freewheeling categories such as vodka have been—partly as a result of the geographical restrictions on where production can take place and partly because, in many instances, the process has never been anything other than craft. Holland and Belgium are still home to a number of wonderful, small-scale, family-run enterprises that remain independent and committed to quality. These guys have been craft distilling for hundreds of years—and, frankly, no one is doing it better.

Van Wees Zeer Oude Genever 15-Year-Old (42% abv)

A. VAN WEES DISTILLERY DE OOIEVAAR, AMSTERDAM, NETHERLANDS

Fenny van Wees is unusual: not only in that she is a female master distiller, but also because she is at the head of Amsterdam's last remaining traditional distillery set in Driehoekstraat, Jordaan, in the heart of the old town. Here, for well over two hundred years, the family-run distillery has been producing its excellent genever.

Until the Seventies, van Wees' forebears supplied the restaurant and bar trade with casks and barrels, but since then—in a bid to reinvigorate the nation's dwindling authentic genever production—the family has been bottling and selling its range and now has a worldwide market.

Above ground, behind a brick-fronted façade in a stillhouse that's the size of a double garage, sit three pot stills and a store room piled high with ingredients—not just the heady sacks of dried citrus peel, spices, and juniper used in Fenny's genever, but also vats of cherries, peaches, and hazelnuts, which are destined for a number of liqueurs. Here, canvas bags of the requisite botanical mix are prepared and weighed out before being deposited in the stills to impart their flavors to the grain alcohol. Fenny runs the three stills simultaneously, nosing the liquid as it runs off, waiting for the perfect cut before the base notes of the botanicals come through.

Underneath the still-room, with a gated-off, locked door, is the distillery's closely guarded hoard: racks of pre-used barrels in which genever is gently maturing (the oldest of which are kept for 20 years). All of the barrels are second-fill, meaning that they have previously matured a different wine or spirit—for the genever, this older wood results in more mellow flavors coming from the barrels; hints of vanilla, spice, and perhaps echoes of the previous liquid inhabitant.

From running the copper pots and nosing the spirits to filling, labeling, and wax-sealing the bottles, Fenny does everything by hand with just a couple of employees to assist her. When you consider the range that A.van Wees produces (see right), this is no mean feat. By all means try the Jonge Genever—it's great—but this place is all about Wees' extra-old spirits. Undoubtedly, the pride of the distillery, the Oude Genever, gently matured for a couple of decades, inhabits a hinterland between gin and whiskey, tasting like a superbly crafted missing link in our liquid history.

Tasting notes: Cheating somewhat, and skipping the entry-level spirits in favor of this refined, oak-aged, Oude-style genever, Wees' Very Old is something quite distinctive and unique for those not yet used to the category. Alongside wonderfully bready, malted-milk characteristics come gentle vanilla, a lilt of pepper and smoked spice, and a rounded, citrus-led sweetness. It's not whiskey; it's not gin—but it is extraordinarily good.
Price: $$$$$
Other products: Jonge Wees; Klarenaer; Loyaal; Loyaal Five-Year-Old; Old Geneva; Rembrandt Korewijn; Roggenaer; Roggenaer Three-Year-Old; Roggenaer 15-Year-Old; Taainagel; Very Old Geneva; Very Old Geneva 10-Year-Old; Very Old Geneva 15-Year-Old; Very Old Van Wees 20-Year-Old; Pure Malt Three-Year-Old; and a range of liqueurs and bitters
Web: de-ooievaar.nl

Dutch and Belgian Genever Distilleries

• Van Wees
• Onder de Boompjes
• Zuidam
• Filliers

Zuidam Zeer Oude Genever (38% abv)

ZUIDAM DISTILLERS, BAARLE NASSAU, NETHERLANDS

Run by brothers Guilbert and Patrick under the watchful eye of father Fred van Zuidam (who founded the distillery in 1975) and mother Hélène (who took on the design of the product packaging in the Eighties), Zuidam Distillers is a resolutely family business—and a successful one at that. Since it opened 30 years ago, it has gone from a one-pot-still operation to the four-still distillery that they run today.

Although there are other products on its books, Zuidam's flagship spirit is its range of exceptional genevers, which it produces in a resolutely craft way—the grain for the malt wine is ground by traditional windmills for crying out loud! Importantly, this is more than just a tourist gimmick: "The traditional millstones of the windmills slowly grind the malted barley into flour. This way of milling causes almost no increase in the temperature of the grain and thus helps preserve the wonderful aromas," the Zuidams explain.

Once the malted barley, rye, and corn flour arrives in the distillery, it is mashed with hot water to release the enzymes and begin the fermentation process; this process lasts around eight hours. The resulting flour soup is fed into tanks, where it bubbles away for five days until fermentation finishes, gently and leisurely developing its malty, yeasty, fruity characteristics. This malt wine is distilled three times in the copper pot stills, which, even though they're small, have a large surface area to promote good contact with the spirit. According to the Zuidams, "This helps to eliminate any unwanted substances and also stimulates the formation of the complex and fruity esters."

Tasting notes: Old-style, but unaged, this is a fine example of the Zuidam's house genever. It has sourdough-bread flavors that meld with a weight of gorgeous juniper spice, which almost tips into an aniseed note. Complex and worth unpicking. If you can't get hold of this iteration, then try the more widely distributed Five-Year-Old—it's a trifle more expensive, and you don't get to sample the more "raw" characteristics of the spirit; with a few years in barrel, it develops caramel, toffee, and spice notes (think candied ginger).

Price: $$$

Other products: Dutch Genever; Jonge Graan Genever; Zeer Oude Genever 1 Jaar; Zeer Oude Genever 2 Jaar; Zeer Oude Genever 3 Jaar; Zeer Oude Genever 5 Jaar; Korenwijn 1 Jaar; Korenwijn 5 Jaar; Korenwijn 10 Jaar; and a range of liqueurs, rum, and whiskey

Web: zuidam.eu

Premium Genever (35% ABV)

ONDER DE BOOMPJES, SCHIEDAM, NETHERLANDS

Not only does it have a fabulous name (which sounds like it should be sung to the tune of The Drifters' "Boardwalk") and a coveted Schiedam location, Boompjes also has an interesting history and heritage. Although its roots date back to genever's heyday in 1658, all is not quite what it seems. The distillery was originally sited in Rotterdam's Waalhaven district where, centuries after its inception, it was facing bankruptcy. In 2010, a former real-estate entrepreneur Jean-Paul Batenburg, who had a long-standing pipe dream to run a spirits company, saw an interesting opportunity—and jumped at it. Consigning the original building to history, Batenburg instead bought the brand name and set about establishing what is effectively a modern craft distillery.

There are four neatly crafted, sleekly packaged products in the Boompjes range, including a gin and a vodka, though it's the Premium Genever and the Old Dutch Genever which are worth our attention. Boompjes is a distillery that's determined to do things properly, and is one of but a handful that ferments its own *moutwijn* ("malt wine") using a recipe that contains one part rye to two parts malted barley. For the Premium Genever, the fermented mash is distilled four times before being rested in stainless-steel tanks. Of course, the malt wine is only part of the story with genever: the neutral spirit with which it is mixed comes from a wheat base and—having been cut with water to around 50 percent—is macerated with the botanicals. Boompjes' recipe for its Premium Genever includes the usual suspects like juniper, angelica, and coriander, but also vanilla and lavender.

The Old Dutch Genever starts with a similar mash bill, but there the similarities end: it is distilled only three times, and combined with a neutral spirit that has been simply macerated with orange peel and juniper before being put into wood. Old Tennessee whiskey barrels are used to mellow the genever for three years before it's bottled.

Tasting notes: Where the Oude-style genevers—and most especially the aged Oude ones—have some of the more robust characteristics that come with malted-grain spirit and age, the small amount of malt wine in this elegant genever means it's more akin to a conventional gin style (or at least it would be were the juniper not so well integrated). Initial sweetness from the spirit sits alongside the vanilla, while the floral, citrus, and pine-like sensations build. Try it mixed in a classic gin cocktail such as an Aviation.

Price: $$

Other products: Old Dutch Genever; Sylvius Gin; Oseven 7 Vodka

Web: onderdeboompjes.eu

Filliers' 38° 5-Year-Old Oude Graanjenever (38% abv)

FILLIERS, BACHTE-MARIA-LEERNE, BELGIUM

Farmers needing to diversify isn't just a 21st-century reaction to reduced subsidies and falling milk prices—in fact, toward the end of the 18th century, Belgian-born Karel Lodewijk Filliers was pushing his family away from their agricultural past and toward its distilling future. (Good move, Karel!) The family took to genever production rather enthusiastically, and a generation later, in 1880, a steam engine was installed to facilitate production, and the foundations of the distillery proper were laid.

Today, Filliers remains an independent, family-run enterprise. Sticking to its well-worn practices, it ferments and distils its own malt wine in copper pots, using a combination of wheat, rye, and malted barley. Then, unusually, the malt wine is aged in wood for three years before it is eventually combined with the distilled botanical spirit that makes up the larger component of the genever. As with many genevers, it's the Oude varieties that stand out: for these, the juniper berry distillates are also aged in wood and then blended. The level of wood management, nosing, and blending that goes into Filliers' aged Oude genevers inches them ever closer to the world of whiskey…

Tasting notes: The wood aging gives this stone-bottled—and, frankly, awesomely packaged—genever a surprisingly vibrant-hued straw color. On the nose, this is more biscuity and toasty than you might expect (think roasted hazelnuts and latte), while on the palate there is far more herbal spice—a citrus lick and a definite aniseed twist.
Price: $$$
Other products: 30° Jenever; 38° 8-Year-Old Oude Graanjenever; 38° 12-Year-Old Oude Graanjenever; 1992 Vintage Graanjenever (2nd Release); Dry Gin 28; Dry Gin 28 Barrel Aged; Dry Gin 28 Seasonal Tangerine Edition; Dry Gin 28 Sloe Gin 2013; and a range of fruit and other liqueurs
Web: filliers.be

Merrylegs Genever-Style Gin (40% abv)

OREGON SPIRIT DISTILLERS, OREGON, USA

The eagle-eyed among you will already have clocked that this distillery is not in Holland. Nor is it in Germany, Flanders, or—in fact—in any enclave of Europe. Nope—instead, it's from craft's own country, the USA, which means it can't technically produce anything that's called genever. However, it can, and most certainly does, produce a genever-style drink that's a great example of the crafted products that are coming to the fore.

Where our Dutch and Belgian offerings have been focused on extremely traditional techniques, careful production of the spirit, and a certain predilection toward aging, Oregon Spirit Distillers takes a more playful and devil-may-care approach to its range

(which includes Absinthe at the more outré end of the spectrum). Set up in 2009 by former bartender Brad Irwin, along with his wife Kathy (who's in charge of the purse strings), OSD has a handful of employees who work alongside the most important team member, a 90 gallon (400 liter) pot still called Loraine.

To make the grain spirit that goes into the young-style, genever-style gin, Irwin uses wheat and barley from Madras-Culver and rye from Due East in Burns. The juniper, too, is locally grown. Once fermented, the malt wine is distilled, infused with botanicals, and then infused once more to create a smooth-drinking, but flavor-packed, spirit.

US Genever Distilleries

• Oregon Spirit

• New York Distilling

Tasting notes: With the sweet-malted-milk creaminess to the fore, Merrylegs conveys a warming palate of citrus, spice, and pine (from the juniper). Well-integrated and great sipping, though would also be incredible in a Sour.
Price: $$
Other products: Oregon Spirit Vodka; One-Eyed Jon Spiced Rum; CW Irwin Straight Bourbon; Ottis Webber Oregon Wheat Whiskey; Wild Card Absinthe
Web: oregonspiritdistillers.com

Chief Gowanus (44% abv)

NEW YORK DISTILLING COMPANY, BROOKLYN, USA

For those who spend their time thinking about, reading about, and drinking about the liquor industry, there are a few names that always make one sit up and take notice: cocktail historian and writer David Wondrich is a case in point—especially in the intriguing context of the creation of an Old Dutch gin.

In 2012, David was chatting to Allen Katz, one of the trio of industry veterans behind the New York Distilling Company, and was pontificating on the merits of an 1809 recipe he had discovered in *The Practical Distiller* for a Dutch-style gin—proof, he ventured, that colonial Americans were into genever. Being that Brooklyn is an old Dutch colony, and with a portion of American rye whiskey at his disposal to tinker with, Katz decided that recreating this particular magic could be an intriguing taste of living history.

And so a new old, Holland-style gin was born. Taking the NYDC's existing rye whiskey—"Our whiskies are still under wraps, but we are very excited about them. We are specializing in rye whiskies, with nearly all of the grain grown under contract with Pedersen Farms in upstate New York," says Tom Potter, the company's co-founder and president—as a starting point, Wondrich and the team sent it back to the pot still to add juniper and hops to the brew. The spirit then underwent a third distillation before being rested in barrels for three months to iron out any wrinkles. The quirky name comes from "Gowanus, great chief of the Canarsees, back in the days when Brooklyn was still Dutch."

"For us, Chief Gowanus is a loving re-creation of an American original," says Potter. "Though the recipe and style were forgotten for more than a hundred years, we are pleased to bring them back to life. The intent may have been simply to mimic a Dutch gin of the early 1800s, but the rye spirit base and simple botanical build of juniper and hops really created an original category of gin, and one that is extremely interesting for modern bartenders. We think that craft distillers can, and ought to be, creative. Sometimes that means appreciating the endeavors of distillers long past, and bringing their forgotten work back to the forefront."

Tasting notes: Very much a genever style on the nose, with plenty of juniper, baked bread, and some spice too. To taste, this has a rounded mouthfeel and plenty of pine character, along with fruit-cake intensity and spice.
Price: $$$$
Other products: Dorothy Parker American Gin; Perry's Tot Navy Strength Gin
Web: nydistilling.com

RUM

Of all the spirits in production, rum is the most instantly evocative of swashbuckling excess and ribaldry, of bumbo and grog, high seas and high spirits. Its tropical origins, its piratical associations, its lawless, rule-less production all lend it a swaggering reputation and an easy, appealing charm.

Undoubtedly, rum has been many different things in its lifetime, with early incarnations damned as "devil's piss" and modern interpretations more likely to draw comparisons to fine whiskey or brandy to be sipped and savored (undeniably, we are lucky to enjoy much better quality rums today).

SPIRIT OF THE SEA

The history of rum is inextricably linked with that of seafarers, most famously in the Navy. Until relatively recently (July 31, 1970, in the British Navy, for example), daily rations of rum were made available to all sailors. The measure was taken either with beer or lime juice and water, and was known as grog. Although this convention is largely consigned to the captain's logbooks, a strong, dark style of Navy rum remains in production to this day.

Whether being served up on deck or mixed with soda in a bar, rum has never fallen out of favor, but it's currently enjoying a real resurgence, especially in some of the more complex styles. Ian Burrell, rum ambassador (AKA "Man With the Best Job Possible"), says: "Rum is currently showing growth around the world—especially in the premium sector.

People are discovering the notion that rums can be sipped as opposed to just being thrown into a simple serve like a rum and Coke."

To better understand this shape-shifting spirit, we need to go back to its origins in the sugar cane industry and learn a little about how it came to be.

How is rum made?
Rum production methods are intrinsically bound up with Europe and the Caribbean's colonial past, with trading routes and sugar plantations, and it is to there we must look for rum's style variations, which are still very much in evidence today. All rum starts life as sugar cane, a saccharine grass crop which is grown for pressing to extract the sweet, sugary juices that go on to be boiled and solidified into the kind of crystals you're used to stirring into tea. A by-product of this process is molasses—a syrupy liquid that (as the early sugar croppers found) is rather useful when it comes to rum production.

Perhaps counter-intuitively, the style of rum made simply from a distillation of the raw sugar cane juice, rhum agricole, is less common, and is generally restricted to those islands which have a history of French colonization (such as Martinique and Guadalupe). Fermenting this unprocessed juice lends the resulting spirit characteristics that sit at the earthy and vegetal end of the spectrum, which can be harder to get a taste for when compared with the in-your-face, ripe-fruity sweetness of other styles.

The concentrated, sticky molasses is a much more common starting-point for rum production. Essentially, the treacle-like molasses is diluted and fermented before being pot- or column-distilled (the former being more frequently found in the Caribbean, while the latter is usually seen in Latin countries). There are plenty of variables in the fermentation of the molasses—whether only wild yeast is used or brewer's yeasts are added, the length of time that it is fermented for, and so on. It can either be a tightly regulated and industrialized process or left rather more to chance. The quality of this ferment will have a resounding impact on the distilled spirit that's eventually made.

Rum can be bottled unaged, virtually straight off the still; it can be aged in a variety of woods and finished in different casks (as for whiskey); or it can be spiced. (See page 72 for more on the different categories.)

Rules and regulations governing rum

A very short entry this as, essentially, there aren't any. Rum can be made anywhere in the world, by pretty much any method, and there are few labeling requirements (why trouble yourself with fripperies such as age statements?). In the EU, there is a minimum bottling strength of 37.5% and a prohibition against adding artificial flavorings.

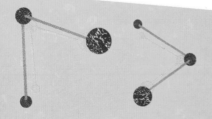

STYLES OF DEMON WATER (RUM, THAT IS)

White or light

As the name implies, this is a clear and light spirit, which is usually made from briefly fermented molasses that is then distilled and rested in stainless steel (rather than aged in barrel). Column distillation is the most common production method for white rum, although artisan and craft chaps tend to prefer pot stills for a bigger flavor. Brazil's Cachaça is one of the most popular styles of light rum.

Spiced

A style of rum that has, of late, become wildly popular—not least because the variety of spices that are added to mellow, golden rum rather obscures the alcohol. Cynics might argue that spiced rums are being pushed toward the more "impressionable" end of the demographic.

Navy

Created to supply the British Admiralty's requirements for rum rations to keep the seamen happy, the dark naval rums were originally distilled in wooden vats rather than the more traditional pot stills (check out Pussers Rum to see these quirks of history still in action). Most modern Navy rums are a combination of column- and pot-distillation, and are at the "potent" end of the spectrum.

Dark

This, the most aged category of rum, has some seriously complex and delectable examples that come laden with flavors of clove and spice, caramel and tropical fruits, stewed fruit and ginger cake (this list goes on…). These spirits can be enjoyed like brandy or Cognac.

Golden

Once again, Sherlock, you'll be able to identify golden rums from their gorgeous, mellow hue. This is the first category of "aged" rums that has spent time in wood, but not as long as dark rum, so it will have less pronounced spices, vanilla, and coconut, which are lent by time in oak. Think bourbon-style sweetness and intensity

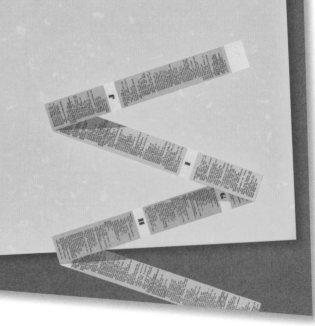

Aging (not so) gracefully

In the cool, damp warehouses of Scotland's mizzle-soaked Highlands, new-make spirit slumbers in its barrels, taking its own good time to interact with the wood. But when you dial up the temperature to "tropical," something quite different occurs. The higher temperature and humidity works on the spirit to draw it rapidly into the grain of the wood, resulting in a high rate of evaporation and aging it in dog years compared with its Celtic brethren. *If* you see an age statement on a bottle of rum (*if* because there's no legal requirement to put one there), then you can be sure you'll enjoy a spirit that will taste like it's seen far longer in wood than you might imagine.

The geography of rum production

There are a number of different territories associated with exceptional rum production, each normally linked to a different style. In the Caribbean, for example, Barbados, Jamaica, and Guyana are renowned for producing rich, complex, "English"-style rums, while Cuba, the Dominican Republic, Trinidad, Panama, Guatemala, and Nicaragua have an inclination toward lighter, whiter, and less obviously aromatic styles. When it comes to modern, craft expressions of rum, though, we are looking to different territories altogether—to North America, Mexico (and so on), and so these older *terroir* distinctions become less relevant. Without doubt, the USA is behind the driving force of the category's revival—thanks in part to rum's historical links with the sugar plantations—and this is where we must look for the new-wave spirits.

Old Ipswich White Cap Rum (40% abv)

TURKEY SHORE DISTILLERIES, MASSACHUSETTS, USA

Most high school history masters are more readily associated with dusty textbooks and elbow patches than rum distilling, but when former teacher Mat Perry decided that a career change was in order, it was the lure of the local area's rum-trading past that began to turn his head.

Over a couple of beers with a long-standing friend (surely how the best-laid plans begin), Mat's idea began to take shape. Delving back into Ipswich's nautical heritage, he discovered that, in the late 18th century, an old distillery had operated on the road he had lived on as a child: Turkey Shore Road. Even more serendipitous was the fact that the cargos of molasses which were shipped in from the West Indies to fuel the rum production were actually offloaded in his backyard, which was the then home of the master distiller. Some things are just meant to be.

Having done some delving into the craft spirit movement, Mat's aforementioned friend, Evan Parker, needed no further persuasion to come on board (leaving his plans for a clam farm in the pipeline): in 2010, the two 30-somethings founded Turkey Shore Distilleries.

Their rum production has a sense of nostalgia about it, combined with a canny understanding of current tastes and markets. Louisiana-produced, top-grade molasses is pumped into the distillery, where it's diluted with water, mixed with yeast, and left to ferment away for a little under a fortnight in four 500-gallon (2,270-liter), open-top fermenters (each of which is named for one of the historic distillery's owners, such as John Heard). It then goes forward into the Kentucky-built copper pot still to be distilled, before either being re-distilled several times (for the white rum), spiced, or decanted into small, charred, white oak barrels for aging (look out for the Tavern Style rum which shows the aged character beautifully).

Tasting notes: Clean, sweetly smooth, and with a crème patisserie vanilla appeal, White Cap is light, elegant, and would make a really superb Daiquiri (the king of rum cocktails, surely).
Other products: Old Ipswich Golden Marsh Spiced Rum; Old Ipswich Greenhead Spiced Rum; Old Ipswich Lab & Cask Reserve Rum; Old Ipswich Tavern Style Rum
Price: $
Web: turkeyshoredistilleries.com

Van Brunt Stillhouse Due North Rum

(40% abv)

VAN BRUNT STILLHOUSE, BROOKLYN, USA

When Daric Schlesselman's not editing nightly news series *The Daily Show*, you might just find him tinkering with the stills or checking a spirit run's quality at his Brooklyn-based distillery, the Van Brunt Stillhouse. Named for Cornelius Van Brunt, one of Brooklyn's Dutch forefathers and a farmer along Gowanus Creek, the name is a nod to the settlers' pioneering spirit (and also the pioneering spirits they brought with them).

"I love the magic of the whole process," says Daric. "I love the wonder of fermentation and the alchemy of distillation. I also love making something with my hands that I can share with people. I get great joy when someone enjoys the fruits of my labor." And enjoy it they do: the distillery's collection of spirits—from grappas to rums—have a dedicated following.

While the grappa was inspired by a stroll past Red Hook Winery—where the surplus of grape skins seemed too good an opportunity to miss—the rum was a pet project that Daric was determined to get right. "Our sugar is a granulated whole sugar cane," he explains. "It's virtually unprocessed. The growers cut it, grind it, and then dry it in the sun in an Ayurvedic process. It retains all its minerals and has a rich bouquet with rich molasses notes because no molasses has been removed." It's also organic and Fair Trade, if you want to drink with an even clearer conscience.

The sugar wash is fermented for about five days before being double distilled—the first time in a pot still and the second in a column to clean it up. The wood recipe is also critical: "Up until recently, we were aging in a variety of barrels, from new, charred, American oak to first-fill, used bourbon casks, as well as some of our own used 10-gallon whiskey casks," Daric explains. But innovation is central to the Van Brunt philosophy. "We have recently pooled all of our rum and created a Solera program; from now on, that's how our rum will be aged." The future for Due North is looking increasingly sophisticated.

Tasting notes: Uncomplicated caramel and toast on the nose; some sweetness, tasty toffee, and dried fruit (apricots?) on the palate, giving way to a surprisingly dry finish.
Other products: Stillhouse Moonshine; Stillhouse Whiskey; and a range of grappas made and released according to market.
Price: $$
Web: vanbruntstillhouse.com

Thomas Tew (42% abv)

NEWPORT DISTILLING CO., RHODE ISLAND, USA

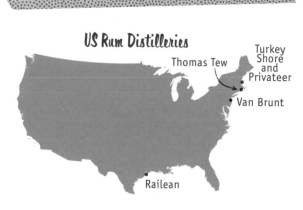

US Rum Distilleries

Thomas Tew

Turkey Shore and Privateer

Van Brunt

Railean

thomas tew

AUTHENTIC POT-STILL
RUM
NEWPORT, RI USA

Brent, Derek, Mark, and Will: four guys who met at school and who really, really liked beer. So do a lot of college students. But this band of brothers decided they liked it so much that, rather than waste too much time on getting great grades in the sciences they were studying, they should focus on researching their pet subject. On graduating, and being faced with the prospect of getting "proper" jobs, they decided it was time to take action and in 1999 Coastal Extreme Brewery (AKA Newport Storm Brewery) was founded.

The brewery flourished and expanded, and off the back of this the four amigos decided to take the next step and set up a distillery that would take their Rhode Island home back to the glory days of rum production (at the end of 1769, there were 22 distilleries in the Newport counties). "With this in mind we thought, hey, this would be a really cool thing to bring back to Rhode Island," says co-founder and head distiller Brent Ryan. The Newport Distilling Co., complete with an impressive 88 gallon (400 liter) CARL copper pot still, opened its doors and rolled in the bourbon barrels in 2007, and Thomas Tew was born.

The boys have created a very traditional style of rum made from backstrap molasses, which is fermented with local water, and then twice distilled in the aforementioned CARL still before being gently aged. (Chances are, this is a rather superior product to those that were being produced when its namesake, the legendary pirate Thomas Tew, was roaming the high seas.) "We thought it was appropriate to name our rum after someone who would have drunk a lot of the spirit, and who was around in Newport's distilling heyday," says Brent.

Newport Distilling Co. majors in beautiful, golden, aged rums. "This is rum that you are taking from the still, aging in the barrel and then taking it out the barrel; what you see is what you get. At least a half of the profile you get in an aged rum is coming from the barrel; the barrel is not only cleaning up the spirit, it's allowing it to oxidize, it's imparting the spice character, the sweetness, as well as the color and the oak flavor. Meanwhile, some of the buttery elements come from the distillate. All of these flavors combine together to make an aged rum." Each batch is aged in its own barrel, lending it a unique flavor profile; against each barrel is recorded the fermentation batch that went forward to be distilled, the distillation dates and distillers, and the final yield—which can vary wildly and shows just how idiosyncratic the aging process can be.

Tasting notes: Take the lid off the Muscovado sugar jar, breathe in deeply, and you'll get a lungful that's reminiscent of this sweetly caramelized, gently spicy rum. Coconut and vanilla, butterscotch and toffee, this is a full-bodied, mouthcoating drop that is best savored on ice or straight. Definitely no mixers required.
Price: $
Other products: Beer, a lot of beer
Web: thomastewrums.com

Small Cask Aged Rum (40% abv)

RAILEAN, TEXAS, USA

Kelly Railean used to sail boats for fun, enjoying the rambunctious social life that came with it, and developing a penchant for rum. Kelly still sails boats for fun, only now, rather than just drinking rum, she also distils it. Kelly isn't your average distiller, mind you—not only is she one of the few females who are single-handedly at the helm of a craft distillery, but she has also spearheaded the resurgence of rum as an all-American spirit, raising its profile and highlighting tax loopholes that mean US-based distilleries have had a rather unfair playing field.

Kelly is keen to point out that in the 1700s, the USA was home to around 60 rum distilleries—a number that dwindled to practically none, thanks to tax breaks given to overseas imports and whiskey becoming far cheaper to produce. Determined to reinvigorate the rum trade, and found the first rum distillery in Texas, Kelly founded her eponymous distillery in 2005.

The quiet shores of Galveston Bay, in San Leon, are now home to her all-American distillery, where everything—from the A-grade molasses (which she ferments herself), through the small oak barrels, to the bottles the rum is eventually packaged in—is proudly made in the USA.

Kelly oversees the production of four kinds of rum, from a white spirit that undergoes multiple distillations to a single-distilled, aged rum, which is matured in diminutive, charred American oak barrels. Kelly uses small barrels so she can maneuver them herself, and so that the spirit takes on the wood's character more readily.

Tasting notes: Aged in first-fill American oak barrels, and bottled one barrel at a time, this small-cask rum will vary from batch to batch. The house style for it, though, hits at burnt caramel, coffee, warm sugar, and a distinctly woody, grown-up character. One to try on the rocks.
Other products: El Perico Reposado; El Perico Silver; Reserve XO Rum; Spiced Rum; White Rum
Price: $
Web: railean.com

Privateer True American Rum (45% abv)

PRIVATEER RUM, IPSWICH, USA

If you want to launch a rum brand, counting at least one seafaring, rum-running privateer among your distant relatives can only be a good thing. So it was for Andrew Cabot, who is six generations on from a forebear that sailed the high seas in pursuit of blood and glory (or, more accurately, as a merchant trading goods, including his own distilled rums).

Andrew has created a distillery, with superb nautical branding, that does things by the craft textbook (no matter how lawless his predecessors may have been). Privateer currently distils two types of rum: an amber, which comes from A-grade molasses, and a silver, which is distilled from sugar cane and boiled brown sugar. A couple of quirks in their fermentation and distilling process marks these guys out as quality: firstly, they ferment for longer and ferment lower, allowing the yeasts to do their thing gently and imparting a rich, integrated flavor to the wash.

The still they use also has a variable number of bubble plates, so that the distillate can be intricately controlled—the master distiller can take a precise fractional cut or create a no-plate, "pot-only" second distillation to produce a darker, heavier, more flavorful rum. Aging takes place in different woods, giving a recipe that combines American, French, and Hungarian oak, each imparting distinct characteristics. Each barrel develops its own personality and so, when it comes to blending, the skill is in getting just the right marriage of flavors. The blended spirit is rested in cask to allow it to integrate before bottling. The uniqueness of the product (not to mention the pride they take in it) is demonstrated by the details recorded for each batch number, so that you can trace precisely which barrels went into your brew.

Tasting notes: On the nose, this light amber rum delivers caramel, tropical-fruit, and candied-orange notes; meanwhile, there's a sweetness and luxe roundness to the mouthfeel. Coconut, caramel, and spice combine to give an elegant finish. Expect (and appreciate!) the batch-to-batch variation.

Other products: Privateer Silver Reserve Rum; Privateer Single Batch Release Gin

Price: $$

Web: privateerrum.com

TEQUILA, AGAVE SPIRITS, AND MEZCAL

To the general public, the most maligned and misunderstood of spirits is tequila. However, for those who in their youth were not put off by over-exuberant experimentations with low-quality examples, it continues to be a perennial favorite. And while tequila is still the most prevalent of the agave-based spirits, new producers, both in Mexico and north of the border, are offering excellent alternatives to the traditional examples coming out of the state of Jalisco.

TEQUILA

Enthusiastic consumers of tequila have been hallooing the cry of "hold the salt and lemon" so loudly and for so long that the message has surely been disseminated throughout the bulk of the agave-juice-consuming community. In the unlikely event that you're yet to be inducted into the sipping, not slamming, contingent, now is the time to start: spirits that are lovingly coaxed from the agave plant and produced with deference to tradition and technique are artisan products which deserve our respect. We'll begin with tequila, putting its hotheaded sibling, mezcal, to one side for a moment. Because it is produced in a strictly geographically delimitated area, tequila has spawned numerous imitators in the craft movement that style themselves as "agave spirit" (or permutations thereof), which are made outside of the Mexican heartland; while some of these merit our attention, we must first turn to the real McCoy.

TEQUILA: WHAT, WHERE, HOW?

Jalisco, Mexico: home to rainforests and plains, mountains and beaches; birthplace of Mariachi music, Jaripeo bull-riding, and, of course, tequila. This world-class spirit, named after a town in the state located in the Los Altos highlands, is famously produced from the juice of blue agave plants and (almost certainly) has its origins in the time of the Aztecs.

Mexican law dictates that agave spirit can only be called tequila if it comes from Jalisco or defined areas in neighboring Guanajuato, Michoacán, Nayarit, and Tamaulipas. All aspects of tequila production are regulated by a body called Norma Oficial Mexicana (NOM), and you'll find its abbreviated initials on bottles of genuine tequila (look out for this information on the label).

Terroir-wise, the tequila production area spans both high and low lands, with soil types that lend their characteristics to the Blue Weber Agave (*Agave tequilana*) from which the spirit is made. Those agaves grown at altitude are renowned for their size and sweetness, while those toward sea level show more aromatic and fragrant characteristics. The agave plant is not, contrary to appearances, a cactus, but is actually part of the Asparagaceae family (until relatively recently it was, in fact, classed as a member of the Lily family).

In favorable conditions—sandy soils and a decent altitude—agaves can grow to around 6½ft (2m) or more. Agaves need careful farming to ensure their suitability for tequila production and agave farmers, who are known as *jimadores*, keep a close watch over individual plants to prevent them flowering. Were nature allowed to take its course, the plant would send up large, dramatic shoots. Although impressive-looking, these draw energy away from the pina, which is the heart of the plant where the essential sap is stored. Agave-growing is not a short-term investment; it can take more than a decade for the pina to reach its optimum size, carbohydrate content, and physical maturity, but—usually in its twelfth year—the pina is harvested and can weigh the equivalent of an average-sized man.

Once harvested, the pinas are sliced into sections before being gently steamed in ovens (these are usually coal- or gas-fired nowadays, but would traditionally have been wood-fired and stone-lined). The cooking process converts the agaves' natural starches into fermentable sugars and can take up to three days, during which time the fibers can gently soften without a risk of burning. The cooking process is one in which the industrial producers part ways with the more artisan ones, the former more often than not opting for a pressure-cooker-style oven, which condenses the steaming time to around 12 hours. Once cooked, the pinas are rested for a day or so before being pulped using a huge grinding stone called a *tahona*—in modern distilleries, this process is replaced with a more efficient (though far less charming) automated milling machine. The crushed fibers are then rinsed with water and this liquid is collected for mixing with yeast (natural yeasts are rarely relied upon) and fermented. Open-top tanks are commonly used and fermentation can take up to a fortnight. Occasionally, the pulped agave is added to the tanks to impart some extra flavors—traditionally, the distillery workers would also have jumped into the tanks to facilitate mixing in the pulp. Thankfully, not all traditions have endured. After fermentation, the low-alcohol tequila wort is double distilled, which takes place either in a pot or column still.

Tequila producers

In the same way that there have traditionally been just a handful of bourbon distilleries, responsible for hundreds of brands, so too is the tequila industry centered around a few umbrella producers who make spirits under a multitude of labels. These are identified on the bottle by a "NOM" code (check out which other brands are made at the same distillery by entering the name into the database at www.tequila.net).

While the distilleries work to the brand's specification and ingredients, and this is a perfectly legitimate process, it's not very craft, so, in the selection provided here, alongside an example of a producer (Sophie Decobecq) who's keeping things artisan while working with Agaveros y Tequileros Unidos de Los Altos, we've also touched on the world of "100 percent agave" spirits, which are small-batch-made outside Mexico.

TYPES OF TEQUILA

Tequila can either be bottled as "100 percent agave" (good) or as a "Mixto" (not so good). A Mixto need only contain a majority share of agave distillate, while the remaining 49 percent can come from any base alcohol. Quality tequilas are rarely anything other than 100 percent agave, so remain eagle-eyed when appraising the label, as this will *always* be stated; if no mention of "100 percent agave" is made, you'll be drinking a Mixto. Tequilas are then classified according to their age, with the main categories being:

Blanco

(AKA "Plata," "Silver," or "White"): These are the youngest tequilas, having only been briefly rested in stainless steel before being bottled within 60 days of distillation. These tequilas are characteristically grassy, fresh, citrusy, herbaceous, and vegetal, and show that youth is no bad thing in a tequila: you get a real taste of the *terroir*.

Reposado (literally meaning "rested")

This style of tequila has been matured for a minimum of two and a maximum of 12 months in wood. As ex-bourbon American oak is often the barrel of choice, flavors of caramel, vanilla, toast, and so on add complexity alongside the vegetal characters that still show through.

Añejo (i.e. aged)

Tequilas that carry this label are naturally richer and deeper in color than their less mature siblings, and have seen wood for at least a year. After 12 months in barrel, they are beginning to pick up more depth and more vanilla, toffee, toasty, and spicy notes from the wood.

Extra Añejo

Used to describe tequilas that have been matured for at least three years, the Extra *Añejo* category is a relative newcomer, having been created in 2006, which coincided remarkably neatly with a rapid growth in the ultra-premium end of the spectrum. As with most spirits, the more you age a spirit, the greater price you can command for it (after all, you've been investing in its maturation, while the angels have been enthusiastically sipping their share). However, it is often argued that rather than continuing to develop depth and breadth, tequila can suffer with age, as it loses some of its earthy freshness. It's a matter of personal choice: older tequila certainly tastes less like tequila, as it begins to adopt more of the smoothly rounded, spiced characteristics that we associate with dark spirits.

Calle 23 Blanco Tequila (40% ABV)

CALLE 23, GUADALAJARA, JALISCO

Sophie Decobecq is not your average tequila producer. Well, she's a "she" for a start. And she's French. And she has degrees in biochemistry and engineering. In the early 2000s, Sophie spent time researching agave production in Mexico and South Africa, developing some serious expertise in tequila production. Once her studies were complete, she returned home to France and to the brandy industry. However, the Mexican spirit had captured her imagination: she wanted to make her own version, using her own distilling nouse.

Moving to Guadalajara, in the highlands of Jalisco, Sophie began to recce the local distilleries, eventually finding one—Agaveros y Tequileros Unidos de Los Altos—which, although it was a producer for more than a dozen other brands, was keen to benefit from her expertise and, most importantly, was happy to help her distil her tequila her way.

The agaves, which are grown at altitude, are selected for optimum fermentable sugars and ripeness; after harvest, they are brought into the distillery, where they're cooked in stainless-steel autoclaves (ovens) for around 15 hours. Once baked, the agaves are fermented—which is not the "natural yeast" process that the mezcal distilleries encourage, but is rather a playground for Sophie's biochemistry knowledge: she matches specific yeast types to the wash depending on the character of the spirit she is producing. During fermentation, she is on hand—equipped with a microscope—to check that the yeast is behaving as she wishes. A slow double distillation then takes place, before the Reposado and Añejo are introduced to American oak, ex-whiskey barrels.

Tasting notes: Light and nuanced, this has an approachable subtlety in its youth. White pepper, cut green bell (sweet) pepper, and a fresh-sharp character akin to Granny Smith apples combine to give a surprisingly complex mouthful.
Price: $
Other products: Calle 23 Añejo Tequila; Calle 23 Reposado Tequila
Web: tequilacalle23.com

100% AGAVE SPIRITS

As yet, beyond the confines of Mexico, the growing and processing of agave are yet to take hold. The three American craft distilleries described here all produce their spirits from imported agave syrup.

El Perico (40% abv)

RAILEAN, TEXAS, USA

Flag-wavingly patriotic, the all-American nature of Kelly Railean's spirits is of central importance to the brand, and she is proud that the production—from fermentation onward—of her ground-breaking agave spirits takes place in Texas. Distilled several times, Railean produces both an unaged and a Reposado style from 100 percent Blue Weber Agave. The result for the former is "a clear and typically unaged smooth spirit, where the true flavors and the intensity of the agave are present, as well as the natural sweetness," she says.

Price: $$
Web: railean.com (see also *Rum*, page 78)

US Agave Spirits Distilleries

- Roundhouse
- Tailwinds
- Railean

Tatanka (40% abv)

ROUNDHOUSE SPIRITS, BOULDER, COLORADO, USA

Among Boulder's craft breweries and wineries, Alex Nelson saw a gap in the market for a boutique distillery. He founded Roundhouse in 2008, bringing on board Ted Palmer as president and distiller. Ted, who had had a glimpse of distilling's illicit pleasures at his grandfather's knee, "had always wanted to be a distiller." They began with a gin, experimenting with age and barrels, and continued to innovate with other products, such as coffee and pumpkin liqueurs. The latest innovation is an agave-based spirit called Tatanka: "We ferment the plants' syrup using a delicate mix of yeasts and Rocky Mountain water, extracting the natural flavors," they say. Currently, only 1,000 bottles have been released, with a Reposado or Añejo to come.

Price: $$
Other products: Imperial Barrel Aged Gin; Roundhouse Gin; Corretto Coffee Liqueur; Pumpkin King Cordial
Web: roundhousespirits.com

Midnight Caye (40% abv)

TAILWINDS DISTILLING, CHICAGO, ILLINOIS, USA

Founded by Toby Beall and his brother Jamey in 2012, Tailwinds was born of their twin passions for home-brewing (turned distilling) and Toby's love of rum (an interest developed during various sorties to the Caribbean in his capacity as a pilot). Located near downtown Chicago, the chaps' distillery is sited in a 5,000 square foot (465 square meter) facility, where they can ferment, distil, age, and offer tastings. Their first foray was into rum—their collection includes three styles—but a more recent experiment brought them to distil agave syrup to create Midnight Caye tequila-style products. "We offer two styles of Midnight Caye: Silver, which embraces the Blue Agave in its purest form, from the still straight to the bottle, and Rested, in which the spirit is allowed to mellow in French oak barrels for some time," they say.

Price: $$$
Other products: Taildragger Amber; Taildragger Coffee; Taildragger Silver
Web: tailwindsdistilling.com

MEZCAL

Mezcal has traditionally been portrayed as tequila's unruly, brawling, chain-smoking, swaggering brother: while it may be less regulated than its Jalisco counterpart, it's certainly no less good—in fact, it's artisan, locally made, and, at its best, quite extraordinary.

A NATIONAL SPIRIT

First then, geography: while tequila production is limited to Jalisco and its surrounding areas, mezcal is produced over a much wider area (since 2003, seven states across Mexico are designated for mezcal production). The state of Oaxaca is considered the pre-eminent area for its production, where it is focused on three valleys that fan out from Oaxaca City, one north, one south, and one heading toward the coast. Within each valley you'll find a distinct microclimate in which the agave is grown, as well as quirky differences in production methods. To complicate matters further, mezcal is not simply produced from one variety of agave (such as tequila's Blue Weber). Instead, almost 30 different types of agave are permitted by the governing body COMERCAM. And, just as different grape varieties will produce different wines, so too will different agaves give different characteristics to the finished spirit.

The two agave varieties you'll need in your lexicon are Espadín and Tobalá. Espadín accounts for the vast majority of mezcal production, not least because it grows quickly and contains plenty of sugars, which makes it especially well suited to distillation. Tobalá is the next best-known variety—although not because it's commonly seen (quite the reverse, in fact). This variety grows wild, and thrives in hard-to-get-to, craggy, shady spots at altitude; as it cannot be cultivated commercially, its rarity is reflected in its price and adds a certain cache to the style. Flavor-wise, it is generally felt to be more fruity and tropical than Espadín.

How mezcal is made

Mezcal's production methods are inherently craft: they are produced to century-old recipes on a small-scale and in a genuinely handmade, artisan way. While the agricultural processes—especially if we are talking about the commercially farmed Espadín agave—are much the same as those used in tequila production, things get more interesting once the pinas have left the farms.

Within mezcal-producing villages, there will often be a center of *fábricas* production houses where the pinas can be prepared and mashed, and their juices distilled. Rather than being steamed in pressure cookers, mezcal agave is made ready for fermentation by baking the pinas in large, stone-lined pits (called *palenques* or *hornos*). Wood fires are lit in the bottom of these pits and, once the stones are hot, the pinas are piled on top, where they are gently cooked for several days, thus imparting smoky flavors and converting the starches into sugars.

Once removed from the pits, the pinas are mashed using a stone grinding wheel, which is similar to the traditional tequila *tahona*, before being fermented.

Mezcal distillation takes its own idiosyncratic form, with producers largely using pot stills, which can be made from clay, ceramic, or copper and can take any shape. Distillations are usually run gently and slowly, and the spirit is distilled twice before being aged.

Mezcal styles

With aging categories that are broadly similar to those of tequila, mezcal's unaged format is known as Joven (rather than Blanco), while Reposado and Añejo cover the more mature spirits. Purists argue that the only way to drink mezcal is unaged. Bottles occasionally contain that rarest of delicacies: a worm. In addition, there is an absolute corker of a category, called Pechuga, which is usually only made to furnish the producer's own table. Pechuga Mezcal is made by re-distilling the spirit with a selection of locally available fruit, nuts, and grains, as well as raw, skinless chicken breast. Yes, chicken.

Del Maguey Vida (42% abv)

DEL MAGUEY SINGLE VILLAGE MEZCALS

Ron Cooper is an artist by vocation—his work is in the permanent collection of NYC's Guggenheim Museum—but he's also a curator of some of the world's most rare and remarkable mezcals. Having established his career in Sixties' Los Angeles, Ron—furnished with cash raised from his artistic successes—swapped California for New Mexico. He established himself in a village where he could work on a weaving project and, while creating his images, also set to work finding the best local mezcal he could.

His dusty adventures along dirt roads in search of the produce of remote villages were frequently rewarded by re-used bottles filled with the most extraordinary spirits. As time went on, and Ron tasted more of the "commercially available" mezcals to be found in bars, he realized he had stumbled upon far better stuff made by real craftsmen. He wanted others to taste this spirit as it truly should be: a traditionally made, integral part of village life.

He set about talking with some of the producers, coaxing them into making a few hundred bottles more, which he then packaged with striking labels to export and sell. Ron now plays the *négociant* role,

acting as the broker that brings these incredibly small-scale, but incredibly impressive, spirits to the market. He's credited with single-handedly raising the mezcal category from an also-ran next to tequila to something that's gaining a dedicated following of fans. As the middle man, Ron can't be credited as a craft producer per se, but he is responsible for bringing Vida, his "entry level" (double-distilled, copper-pot-made) spirit to market, along with those from village producers, detailed here.

Tasting notes: On the nose this has lovely, vegetal, agave notes; to taste, this savory characteristic combines intriguingly with tinned tangerines, a honeyed perfume, and baked spices.
Price: $$
Other products: Chichicapa; Del Maguey Crema de Mezcal; Minero Santa Catarina Minas; Pechuga; San Luis Del Rio; Santo Domingo Albarradas; 100% Tobala
Web: delmaguey.com

Pierde Almas Espadín Mezcal (51% abv)

PIERDE ALMAS, OAXACA, MEXICO

The project of another artist (what is it about mezcal?), Pierde Almas is owned and run by American-born painter Jonathan Barbieri, who has lived in Oaxaca for more than three decades. He works with the Sanchez family to produce a boutique range of mezcals and a particularly unusual mezcal-gin hybrid.

The *palenque* ("distillery") is located in the village of San Baltazar Chichicapam, where it is operated in much the same way as it would have been for hundreds of years (give or take the odd marketing strategy). The oak used to fuel the fires that bake the maguey is foraged; the agave is milled by a horse-drawn wheel; fermentation is slow and painstaking, taking up to a week; distillation happens in a Moorish-style alembic still; and the spirit is twice distilled. Wood-aging is frowned upon: this artisan spirit should, they say, be consumed in its unadulterated form.

There is plenty of variation in the products produced, with "consistency, not uniformity" being key: the three varieties of agave used are converted to differing alcohol strengths, and lend subtly discernible flavors

to the spirit (apparently, even the weather can make a difference to how the fermentation runs, when everything is kept 100 percent natural and chemical-free). Pierde Almas's hand-crafted touch is continued right through to the bottling and labeling: the paper for the labels is handmade using the distillery's discarded agave fibers (among others) and the labels then hand-printed before being fixed to clear, Bordeaux-style bottles. The effect is rustic, yes, but stylishly so.

Tasting notes: An unaged spirit, this is clean and clear, with a delectably wood-smoke-scented nose. There's a floral, vegetal note, which becomes more pronounced on the palate; there's a mouthwatering freshness that is part citrus and part herbal.
Price: $$$$
Other products: Dobadaán Mezcal; Pechuga; Puritita Verdá; Tobaziche Mezcal
Web: pierdealmas.com

Fidencio Único (40% abv)

FIDENCIO SPIRITS, OAXACA, MEXICO

Fidencio has a story that begins generations ago; equally, it is a tale of modern investment and a smart business partnership. The more conventionally romantic portion of the tale began with Enrique Jimenez's forebears, who started making mezcal over 100 years ago in Santiago Matatlán, Oaxaca. Four generations on, via a degree in chemical engineering, Enrique was ready both to take on the family trade as a *mezcalero*, but on his own terms. He had a vision to create Único, a mezcal that was a pure expression of the agave, biodynamically produced (the agave is harvested during a new moon for clarity of flavor).

Enrique set about designing and building his own distillery, somewhere he could produce a range of mezcals (such as the Clasico and Pechuga expressions) using traditional methods—for example, the *tahona*-crushing wheel would still, literally, be horse-powered by the willing Rocio—but also be creative and experiment with new ideas, such as the radiant oven he uses to produce Único. Where traditional producers rely on fire-fueled pits to roast their agave, Enrique's method for Único is more akin to tequila production with a dry radiant heat source that's able to break down the starches in the agave without introducing charred notes to the pina.

Meanwhile, in 2007, while Enrique was busily planning and building, a former bartender Amy had discovered a hotel in disrepair (called Villas Carrizalillo) while travelling through Oaxaca. She decided to take it on. A former colleague and friend, Arik, came to visit and they were both, they explain, bitten by the mezcal bug. Arik decided he wanted to get involved. Mutual friends introduced Amy and Arik to Enrique—they loved what he was doing; Enrique was drawn to their industry insights. The timing was serendipitous; Enrique's distillery was ready to roll, and soon their fantastically linear, beautifully crafted spirit came off the still.

Tasting notes: Another unaged spirit, made from 100 percent organically produced agave, this is crisp and clean on the nose, and crystal clear. It's got an asparagus-like, vegetal, earthy quality that sits alongside a hint of fruity complexity.
Price: $$
Other products: Fidencio Clásico; Fidencio Pechuga, Fidencio Tobalá, Fidencio Madrecuixe, Fidencio Tepextate, Fidencio Tierra Blanca
Web: fidenciomezcal.com

Mexican Tequila and Mezcal Distilleries

• Calle 23

Ilegal

Del Maguay — Fidencio

Pierde Almas

Ilegal Joven (40% abv)

ILEGAL MEZCAL, OAXACA, MEXICO

Undoubtedly one of the best things about Ilegal Mezcal—and there are a lot to choose from—is its hedonistic, morally dubious backstory which is tinged with just enough wrong-side-of-the-law activity to make it grubbily appealing. Conceived in 2004 by John Rexer, who owns a notorious, eclectic dive bar called Café No Sé in Antigua Guatemala, Ilegal (the brand) started life, not as one mezcal from one producer, but rather as the nickname for bootlegged spirit sourced from village producers in Oaxaca, which John managed to get over the border.

Needing enough booze to service his dedicated mezcal bar, accessed behind a beaten-up fridge door (what else?), meant John's spirit-running trips were frequent, and not without incident—being robbed, paying bribes, adopting a disguise as a priest, and so on. One of his regular suppliers in Oaxaca suggested that he bought from him on a bigger scale (he "had an uncle" who could help with import issues); it was a good opportunity, and John decided that, not only would he buy more from this producer, but he would also buy better—commissioning the spirit to be exactly as he wanted Ilegal to taste.

The mezcal they bottle is certainly worthy of its unconventional brand story: it's traditionally produced from 100 percent agave, mainly the Espadín variety, which is pit-roasted the old-fashioned way. Horses are used to turn the grinding wheel, and fermentation relies on natural yeasts (which means it takes as long as it takes) before the wash is small-batch-distilled.

Going slightly against the trend in boutique mezcal, Ilegal have happily released some aged products too, with a four-month rested Reposado and a 13-month matured Añejo (American oak is used for both). Ilegal Joven, though, is still where it's at for the purists.

Tasting notes: Wood smoke, pepper, and citrus on the nose; to taste, this is a bright, but intense, hit of herbaceous agave with a pleasant, creamy finish.
Price: $$$
Other products: Ilegal Mezcal Añejo and Ilegal Mezcal Reposado
Web: ilegalmezcal.com

SINGLE MALT WHISKY

The product of just one distillery and just one type of grain, single malt whisky has a beautiful linearity to it: each spirit born to this category tells its own very specific and very characterful story. When you think of traditionally made Scotch, you might assume that the older the spirit, the more of a liquid narrative it would have to relay, and the more nuanced and exciting it would be, but this isn't necessarily the case when it comes to craft. In the micro-distilling world, some of the most fascinating drams have been made in relatively recent times—all thanks to the creativity and ingenuity of some remarkable distillers across the world.

SCOTCHING THE STATUS QUO

But, before we move on to new distillers on the block, it's worth taking stock of the established scene, specifically in Scotland, and how—or perhaps if—these bastions of beautiful booze should be included in the craft category. After all, just because someone has been small-batch distilling for centuries, this doesn't make them less of a craft distiller, does it?

In introducing this book we looked at the criteria for craft. Though scale is a consideration, remaining diminutive is not essential; though philosophy is key, it is also hard to define; independence, though, is critical. Being independently owned (with no need to account for or justify decisions to "the man") is vital, not only to promote the entrepreneurial spirit that's the life-blood of the movement, but also to give producers the ultimate creative freedom they need to thrive. In Scotland, while a minority of independent, single malt producers remain, the vast majority of loved-and-lauded malt brands shelter under the wing of a much larger distilling giant (Diageo being by far the biggest, owning over 100 whisky brands worldwide at the last count, with Pernod Ricard and Edrington not so far behind).

A handful of distilleries, though, remain family- or founder-run—and this is especially true of the most recently established, which are most certainly cut from craft cloth—more on these shortly. Widening the focus beyond the highlands, islands, and lowlands, single malt is a category that has been fully embraced and reimagined by craft distillers worldwide—perhaps it is the sense of *terroir* that's integral to the spirit, or the purity of the expression that can be created, but whether you head to the land of fire and ice or travel down under to the wilds of Tasmania, you'll find committed producers making some sublime spirits.

Scottish rules: single malt's motherland

While single malt whisk(e)y can be produced anywhere in the world, Scottish single malt whisky (note, no "e")—or Scotch—undoubtedly sets the standard by which others should be judged. Made according to a stringently enforced set of rules to ensure that the quality of the product is protected, styles can vary from a kippery-slap-in-the-face dram that reels with salt and sea through to a honeyed nectar that seduces the drinker.

So, the rules of production, which have been outlined in law since the early 20th century, are: the whisky must be made with malted barley and distilled in Scotland from water and malted barley using copper pot stills (two are usually used). It must be distilled at less than 94.8% and then matured in casks not exceeding 154 gallons (700 liters). It then has to be aged for no less than three years before bottling. Nothing, other than water (and caramel coloring), may be added and it must have a minimum alcoholic strength by volume of 40%.

The Scottish whisky bodies are tigerish in checking that these regulations are met to ensure the reputation of Scotch is protected worldwide. But this is not to say that those outside Scotland, who have taken inspiration from these rules and riffed on them, are doing a bad thing—far from it. Some of the results stemming from this kind of creativity are extremely impressive.

Some notes on production

While you're well-versed in the pot-distilling techniques, it's worth keeping in mind a couple of production points that are especially pertinent to the single malt process, namely the traditional malting floor and the role that peat has to play. These days, seeing a malting floor at an old-school distillery is an increasingly rare thing, as this work is usually subcontracted out to professional maltsters, but the idea of malting your own barley is something that many craft distillers view as vital to their "grain-to-glass" integrity.

Cue the resurgence in traditional malting floors. These are, essentially, large covered barns or sheds where the newly harvested, water-steeped barley can be spread out and heaped into little furrows—as in a ploughed field—by the malt men and their spades. It is turned at regular intervals to ensure that all the grain has access to both the air at the top of the pile and the damp, dark warmth of the bottom to promote healthy, even germination. The grain languishes here, being gently turned, for around five days until the malt men are happy with it.

Now thoughts turn skyward to the iconic part of the malt house building: its numerous pointed or "pagoda" chimneys, which are key to the grain's next stage. In order to prevent it germinating, the grain is spread in a thin layer across another floor inside a kiln, and a fire made with peat or other types of fuel lit underneath to smoke the grain and impart its flavor. Where peat is used, the smoke given off contains chemicals called phenols, which contribute "peaty" characteristics. The longer the barley is exposed, and the smokier the fire, the higher the level of phenols it will absorb. For distillers who use this method, the level of phenols is an essential part of their whisky recipe, and is measured in PPM (phenol parts per million). In commercial whiskies, the highest levels of phenols are found in island Scotch such as Laphroaig and Ardbeg, where steps are taken to maintain their levels, even after the distillation of the spirit has taken place. If you're not sure what phenols taste like, then a measure of either of these whiskies will leave you in little doubt.

United Kingdom Scotch Distilleries

Kilchoman

Penderyn

English Whisky Co

Penderyn Madeira Single Malt (46% abv)

PENDERYN DISTILLERY, BRECON BEACONS, WALES

Anyone who has spent time in Wales's capital city, Cardiff, cannot help but have come across the fine work of brewers S.A. Brain & Co ("All beer has heads, only ours has Brains," etc.). This much-loved institution has an integral part to play in Wales's *wysgi* ("whisky"), Penderyn, the story of which continues some 48km (30 miles) north-west of Cardiff in the foothills of the Brecon Beacons.

Founded in 1998, Penderyn was the first company to distil a Welsh whisky in more than 100 years—which seems extraordinary when you consider the enthusiasm other Celtic nations have for the spirit (blame lies at the door of the Welsh temperance movement). Establishing a new industry means, of course, that you get to invent your own rulebook, and one of the first things Penderyn did was, as we've mentioned, employ the services of Brains brewery. Unlike in Scotland, where your malted barley must—by law—be fermented on site, there's no such regulation in Wales, and so Penderyn's (now former) master distiller Gillian MacDonald was able to commission Brains to produce a malted barley beer, brewed to 8.0% and to Penderyn's exact specifications.

This wasn't the only thing the company was to do differently. Its still is something quite unique—a hybrid between a conventional pot still and a fractional-distillation column still, it was invented for the Welsh company by Dr. David Faraday, descendant of the ground-breaking Victorian scientist, Michael Faraday. The main belly of the pot is charged with the wash, where it is heated until it evaporates and hits a series of plates above, causing condensed fractions to drop back into the pot. The resulting liquid that eventually drips into the spirits safe is a remarkably high alcoholic proof—around 92%—which would be impossible to achieve with a conventional pot. This gives Penderyn an especially pure, especially clean, and especially light spirit—it also adds to its rarity, the tiny cut giving only a barrel of whisky a day.

Tasting notes: Proud holder of the title of Best World Whisky (it won gold medals at both the 2012 and 2013 International Whisky Competitions), you should come to this dram with a certain weight of expectation. On the nose, there's a hint of Werther's Originals, or even condensed-milk sweetness, along with a fruit-cake richness. To taste, there's a "foam-banana," candied element, along with toffee-apple and dried-fruit notes that perhaps come from the Madeira cask finish. Smooth, tasty, and satisfying.

Price: $$$$

Other products: Penderyn Icons of Wales; Penderyn Peated; Penderyn Sherrywood; Brecon Gin; Merlyn Welsh Cream Liqueur; Five Vodka

Web: welsh-whisky.co.uk

When it comes to aging the spirit, things don't get any more conventional. Here, industry guru Jim Swan was brought in to advise, and created a two-barrel aging process: first the new-make is mellowed in ex-bourbon casks from Buffalo Trace and then it is finished in old Madeira casks. Other woods are also used occasionally to create special editions—keep an eye out for new releases. The whisky is aged for at least three years before being cut with the lovely Brecon water, which is drawn from a borehole in the distillery grounds, and then labeled with the exact month and year of production. (There is definite batch-to-batch variation, so this is a necessary and useful addition—check out the scores in Jim Murray's *Whisky Bible* for more).

Kilchoman's 100 Percent Islay (50% abv)

KILCHOMAN DISTILLERY, ISLAY, SCOTLAND

Those who are not familiar with this wind-whipped, rugged little Scottish isle should go immediately to a liquor retailer and buy a bottle of whisky that hails from its shores because tasting the waft of antiseptic ointment, the crash of smoke and peat, the slap of seaweed and saline, and the warm, deep thread that runs through it—from whichever distillery you choose—evokes a sense of place in a way that words simply can't. Some of the most glorious whiskies in the world come from this spot.

While many of Islay's oldest distilleries sit along the fringes of its coastline, its newest—Kilchoman—is a farm distillery sited inland and the first to be built on Islay in 125 years. When, a decade ago, Kilchoman opened its doors (Cask No.1 was filled on December 14, 2005), its founder, Anthony Wills, was seemingly unaware of the craft tide that was rising around him. Instead, he had decided to open his own distillery, having seen the burgeoning enthusiasm for rare and unusual bottlings in the single malt business. With his own farm distillery, he reasoned, a hand-crafted, niche whisky would be able to cater to just such a market.

Having found the location for the farm, Rookside Farm on Islay's West Coast, and knocked on numerous doors to raise the initial capital of a million quid to get started, Anthony and wife Kathy set about sowing the seeds—literally—for the enterprise. Originally, they planted the farm with Optic barley, before changing to the more rugged and robust Publican variety, which was better suited to Islay's temperamental climes. (The farm is able to supply much of the required barley for its whisky, with the balance, which is distilled separately, coming from Port Ellen Maltings).

The distillery is one of only six in Scotland to carry out its own malting: once harvested, the barley is steeped overnight and rested before being spread out over the floor, where it is then left to sprout for five or so days, being turned all the while. It is then smoked over a peaty fire for around 10 hours to achieve phenols of between 20–25ppm. It is then completely dried out for another two days or so before being milled and mashed, and beginning its journey through the pot stills and into barrel. Kilchoman's wood—a vital ingredient in the malt whisky—comes from used casks from the Buffalo Trace Distillery in Kentucky and Oloroso sherry butts from Jerez in Spain.

Tasting notes: For the price, you might expect to sip liquid gold, as this is certainly at the top end of the spectrum for a whisky in the flushes of such relative youth, but, in buying a bottle, you are also buying into the idea of the distillery and its potential to deliver richly with future releases. While 100% Islay is a lightweight when tasted in the context of the range as a whole, its lightly peated style lends it elegance and freshness: this is still a resoundingly delicious single malt with whispers of citrus and barley, sweet hay, and a crunch of pepper. Remarkable stuff.

Price: $$$$$

Other products: Loch Gorm; Machir Bay; and single-cask and vintage releases.

Web: kilchomandistillery.com

St George's Single Malt Whisky
Chapter 15 (46% abv)

THE ENGLISH WHISKY CO., NORFOLK, ENGLAND

Back in 2006, like a North Sea weather system, a storm of hype and publicity was beginning to build over the Norfolk Broads on England's east coast. Word had gotten out that ground had been broken on the first dedicated English whisky distillery to be built in decades: critics, spirits aficionados, and collectors couldn't wait to get a piece of it. Three years later, The English Whisky Co. produced its first sell-out release and made news around the world. But, as founder and farmer Andrew Nelstrop explains, it's not about selling one bottle—that bit is easy if you're a novelty; it's about selling the second, the third, and the subsequent ones after that. Then you know you've got a product worth having. St George's Single Malt is most certainly that.

The English Whisky Co. came about as something of a happy accident. Having been part of a farming family for generations, Andrew started looking into the idea of a running a little whisky still as an interesting retirement project for his father James. "Originally we were going to do a very small micro-distillery, like you see with the breweries in pubs, but back when we decided to do it, in 2006, there was still a minimum still size rule imposed by Customs (which is why there hasn't been a rash of micro-distilleries in the same way as there has in other countries)." What emerged, instead, was something rather more significant, and rather more exciting.

Customs was willing to grant a licence for a larger operation; one larger even than many Scottish distilleries, with stills of more than 396 gallons (1,800 liters). The Nelstrops were undeterred by the scale of the project, and called on the expertise of still-makers Forsyths. In doing so, they were also introduced to Iain Henderson, a Scotsman of legendary distilling pedigree who had headed up Laphroaig's production. Although theoretically retired, Iain was coaxed away from the lure of a more relaxed lifestyle to come south of the border to help establish the Nelstrop's distillery. His experience was immediately put into action, assisting with the set-up—naturally—but also with the recruitment of former Greene King brewer David Fitt, who was to be trained as his successor. ("Iain had spent a lifetime distilling, and David had spent a lifetime brewing, so between them it worked very well," says Andrew.)

The distillery set-up is distinctly low-fi (production is done by hand and nose, rather than computer) and, thanks to its farming founders, is reassuringly grain to glass. While the distillery doesn't grow or malt its own barley—it hardly needs to, as East Anglia's farmers and maltings supply 60 percent of the Scottish whisky industry's requirements—their grain is exclusively locally sourced from Crisp Malting Group, in Fakenham. Water, both for distilling and reducing the spirit, is equally richly abundant: the site is located atop the Breckland aquifer, the eastern reach of the "chalk belt" that runs across England, causing springs, lakes, and streams to bubble to the surface. With the situation and set-up so seemingly perfect, the question is less "Why make English whisky?" and more "Why has it taken so long?"

In its first year, the company made 29 barrels of English whisky. By August 2007, the public could come and see it in production as the visitor center (which now welcomes around 45,000 people a year) opened its doors. They are not, by any means, all whisky lovers, but those who come out of curiosity cannot help but leave with a newly found respect for the spirit. The critics need little convincing as to this East Anglian spirit: the San Francisco World Spirits

Competition, the International Wine & Spirit Competition (IWSC), Jim Murray's *Whisky Bible*, and more rate the dram's being produced as truly exceptional. It's important, here, to look at one of the lessons taught by Iain: that they shouldn't restrict themselves to just one iteration: instead, the English Whisky Co. releases "chapters" when they are ready, each a new expression, age, and finish. While some can now only be found in the most connected of collectors' collections, there are plenty more that are yet to be released. And, with the grace and complexity that comes with age, this means that, surely, the best are yet to come.

Tasting notes: Chapter to chapter, these whiskies are totally different beasts, ranging from light and citrusy to bonfire-night smoked, so consult the relevant tasting notes from the distillery before committing your money to a purchase. This particular instalment, a five-year-old matured in ex-bourbon casks, comes with something of an Asian-spiced element: lemongrass, and lemon balm, ginger and citrus strike you on the nose before the peaty notes manifest themselves (free from the Islay antiseptic notes; this is more akin to wood smoke). This is temptingly moreish—be warned.

Price: $$$$

Other products: A number of other "chapters" are currently available; Nelstrop's Pedro Ximenez; Norfolk Blackberry Liqueur; Norfolk Cream English Malt Spirit; Norfolk Nog English Malt Spirit

Web: englishwhisky.co.uk

Balcones Texas Single Malt (53% abv)

BALCONES, TEXAS, USA

The best whisky in the world—if you're going to weigh such things out in awards and accolades—doesn't flow from an ancient Scottish still or spend its winters maturing in a Kentucky warehouse: instead, it comes from under a bridge in Waco, Texas, the beautiful fruition of one luxuriantly bearded man's dream to become a craft distiller.

Chip Tate, owner of the aforementioned beard, is the architect of this extraordinary enterprise. Using a start-up fund of around $10,000 (consider that many distilleries would need to add an extra three zeros to that sum to accurately account for their investment), he set about getting his hands on a suitable piece of real estate—a welding shop—where he could build his own stills and launch his own whisky. Oh yes, you did read that right: *build his own stills* (craft distilling doesn't get much more craft that that now, does it?). "We cut 'em, pounded 'em out, welded 'em—and they accidentally become a really key part of how we make whisky. There's a specificity to an artist's tools that really can help you craft at your best," says Tate, with a seemingly typical blend of matter-of-fact practicality and creative flair.

United States Scotch Distilleries

Balcones

Tasting notes: Ever so easy on the nose, this is reminiscent of baked pear upside-down cake, caramelized sugar, and *tarte tatin*, which gives way to bread and butter pudding on the palate—a touch of yeast along with quite sophisticated citrus flavors of candied orange and honey. Mellow and delicious.
Price: $$$$$
Other products: Balcones Baby Blue Corn Whisky; Balcones Brimstone Corn Whisky; Balcones Rumble; Balcones Rumble Cask Reserve; Balcones True Blue Cask Strength Corn Whisky; Balcones True Blue 100 Proof Corn Whisky
Web: balconesdistilling.com

The original plan, Tate explains, was to build a brewery—but life, and its various complications, delayed his scheme, which had been 10 years in the making. Plan B, the distillery, came as more of a lightning-bolt idea, but, once inspiration had struck, Tate threw himself into the enterprise: as a result Balcones took shape in the space of weeks, not years.

Rumble, the first spirit produced, had its roots—like the distillery—firmly in Texas. Defying categorization, it was inspired by the thick, local, wild honey, ripe figs, sugar,

and natural Texas Hill Country spring water. More conventional fare came in the form of his Balcones Baby Blue, which was made with an heirloom variety of blue corn from New Mexico. But Tate really, really wanted to produce a single malt that followed more in the tradition of Scotch whisky (perhaps thanks to time spent at the Bruichladdich distillery). Using Golden Promise malted barley, American and French barrels re-coopered to his specifications, and the desert cold nights and scorching hot days that speed maturation, this is exactly what he went on to do.

Combining the barrels and selecting the perfect combination of flavors is where the real art of distilling lies explains Tate: "How those barrels are blended and guided is fundamental; one of the most important things that people don't think about with this job is smell memory—it's very like composing: can you read music in four or five parts and hear what's going to happen?" Tate evidently can—and the results speak for themselves.

Sullivans Cove French Oak Port Cask (47.5% abv)

SULLIVANS COVE, TASMANIA, AUSTRALIA

Australian Scotch Distilleries

Sullivan's Cove

If you really zoom out on a map of the world, you can see just how far apart, geographically at least, Tasmania and Scotland actually are. However, with its remote lakes and hills, springs and peat bogs, and cool weather patterns Tazzie is climactically not so far removed at all… The island's foundling distilling community certainly believe that its burgeoning success is, in part, dependent on these important climactic considerations. Equally, the local brewing heritage, which has cultivated a rich supply of barley, has a vital role to play.

The renaissance in Tasmanian whisky is a mere 20-something years old, with nine distilleries having opened their doors since prohibition was renounced, some 150 years after it was first put in place by the then-Governor John Franklin. The flagship of these is Sullivans Cove, which is still reeling from having been awarded the title of The World's Best Single Malt Whisky at the World Whisky Awards 2014.

Headed up by distiller (and now owner) Patrick Maguire—whose predecessors arrived on these shores at Her Majesty's pleasure, hence the motto "made with conviction"—the distillery was founded in 1994. Maguire led a buy-out of the distillery in 2003, and has nurtured it to its current position. He selects only Tasmanian-grown barley, which gives a markedly "fat" and oily spirit, along with the cleanest water in the world (pretty good raw ingredients)—and essential to conveying the sense of *terroir* Maguire is determined to get across with his whisky.

The island's most celebrated brewery, Cascade, malts the barley for Sullivans Cove before it is fermented into a wash by head brewer Richard Badcock. On reaching the distillery, this beer is double distilled before being put into both ex-bourbon barrels and also French oak. Large barrels (44–66 gallons/200–300 liters) are used, and the whisky is given plenty of time to take on the character of the wood. While smaller barrels speed maturation, Maguire is a firm believer in giving the spirit the time it needs.

Tasting notes: For those lucky enough to get their hands on this now-rare bottling (at time of press, there was a two-month waiting list), you are in for a treat: a really noticeable point of difference with this lush whisky is its full, oleaginous mouthfeel. This is wonderfully rich, with creamy toffee and mature fruit cake on the palate; spice and pepper play their part too.
Price: $$$$$
Other products: American Oak Bourbon Cask Whisky; Double Cask
Web: www.sullivanscovewhisky.com

Once it has reached a lovely, mellow maturity from the barrels, the whisky needs to be reduced in strength by the addition of more of that beautifully clean water; Maguire is quick to stress that non-chill filtering is considered to be vital to keep the most delicate and flavourful oils in the liquid. Instead, it is given a period of several months to settle, so that the alcohol and water can integrate.

BOURBON

In spring 2014, bourbon celebrated an important birthday: half a century had passed since an American Congressional Declaration pronounced the spirit a "distinctive product of the US." From where we sit now, it seems unlikely that bourbon could ever have been regarded otherwise, rooted as it is in USA culture and with its spiritual home literally in Kentucky horse country.

THE GREAT AMERICAN SPIRIT

Pronounced "burr-bun" (not, British friends, "bore-bon" like the biscuit), there are a number of regulations that preside over its production and make it distinct from regular whiskey. Firstly, bourbon must be made in the USA—it's not restricted to the Commonwealth of Kentucky, but a quirk in the law means this is the only state that can declare its name on the label. It must also be made using a specific mash bill that uses between 51 percent and 75 percent corn, a portion of malted barley, and, usually, either wheat or rye (with these last included in whatever quantities the distiller so wishes).

Bourbon must also be distilled to not more than 80% proof—though less than this is usual anyway, and reduced to below 62.5% before it goes into barrel. Then, when it comes to filling, it must be bottled at 40% or more. The barrels used to age bourbon have to be made from new charred oak—much to the relief of the rest of the whisk(e)y industry, which relies

heavily on the second-hand market from these once-used barrels. Lastly, bourbon needs to be "straight"—i.e. made without artificial colors, flavorings, or anything (basically) that doesn't arise naturally from the mash bill, plus yeast, plus water.

While a few short years ago, the majority of us may have labored under the illusion that bourbon could only come from Kentucky—it is, after all, home to the Julep-swigging Derby, to the annual Bourbon Festival, and to the key commercial distilleries—the arrival of craft bourbons has blown fresh air through the category, opening it wide to those wanting to try their hand at producing the sweet, spicy, smooth-drinking style. While previously, just eight distillers—Brown Forman, Buffalo Trace, Four Roses, Heaven Hill, Jim Beam, Maker's Mark, Tom Moore, and Wild Turkey—were responsible for making the several hundred bourbons on the market, nowadays, distillers from across the USA are trying their hand, some with outstanding results. Bourbon is no longer simply a product of the South.

Sour mash

A key element of the bourbon production process is that of sour mashing, one that has been used for nearly two hundred years. You may recognize the name as it appears prominently on the label of arguably America's most famous whiskey, Jack Daniels, which is actually a Tennessee whiskey rather than a bourbon. Confused? Don't be. Tennessee whiskey is very similar to bourbon, but with two subtle differences: firstly, it's made in Tennessee; secondly, it's charcoal filtered before the aging process begins.

The vast majority of American whiskeys are created using the sour mash method. How it works is the distiller takes some of the leftover mash (20% is common practice) from a previous batch of whiskey and adds it to the new grain bill. It's a similar technique that many bakers use for sourdough bread or that beer brewers use to create sour beers.

So how will sour mash affect the bourbon? What it does is help the distiller to achieve a consistency in the taste of the finished product. The yeast strains in the sour mash will have distinct flavor characteristics that make each expression unique. Although there are other elements present during the brewing process that will have an impact on the finished product, sour mashing guarantees that some of the flavor-giving yeast strain from the last distillation is present in the next batch. It is also believed that sour mash encourages fermentation as it reduces the pH of the new mash to levels where yeast strains will thrive.

Hudson Four Grain Bourbon Whiskey (48% abv)

TUTHILLTOWN SPIRITS, NEW YORK, USA

Tuthilltown distillery is a beacon for the craft movement: its hand-crafted spirits are made in a hand-crafted distillery by guys possessed with an enthusiasm that runs off the stills alongside the incredible liquor. There's no need to exaggerate Tuthilltown's craft credentials: these folks could have written the book.

Over a decade ago, Ralph Erenzo dreamt of running a climbers' ranch, and set about purchasing a site in the Hudson Valley hamlet of Gardiner. Fate (or highly vocal local opposition, however you prefer to look at it) stepped in, and so his ranching plans ground to a halt. Perhaps it's the climbers' mentality, but Ralph was far from beaten: he just found a different dream to follow. In 2004, along with business partner and engineer-slash-Windsor-chair-maker Brian Lee, Ralph set about building the first distillery to operate in New York State since the stills ran dry in the Prohibition era.

"There was no manual for how to build a small distillery—so we decided to do it all ourselves," says Ralph—and they sure did. The centuries-old grist-mill building was renovated and retro-fitted and, from wiring the electricity to painting the clapboard, the project was a learn-on-the-job labor of love. "Climbing really gave me a hand along," says Ralph. "It taught me that I could do a lot more than I thought." Aside from sinking the well and operating the crane that lifted the stills through the roof, the Tuthilltown boys put together the whole shebang from scratch.

Three years of graft, being on the job 24 hours a day when needed, and no holiday was integral to their success. When the first spirit ran off the German-imported stills—they initially fermented and distilled unwanted local apples to make vodka and apple brandy—they knew they were on to a good thing. Before long, the more nuanced challenge of making a grain spirit began to occupy Ralph's thoughts. "Whiskey came to us after a while when we began to get a little tired of simply making a high-proof spirit," he says.

Whether we're talking about the grain (which comes, largely, from within a 3 mile/5 km radius), or the staff ("they've all learned on the job"), Tuthilltown is resolutely New York State local. It's the key to the spirit,

says distiller Joel Elder: "If you use a better grain for bread, you'll get a better bread. Exactly the same is true of whiskey." For the Four Grain Bourbon, the mash bill—as you would expect—includes corn, rye, wheat, and malted barley. Around 800lb (363kg) of it is brought into the distillery, where it is ground on site, then mashed and fermented in 200-gallon (900-liter) open-top fermenters. Then, having been twice distilled, it goes into small barrels to begin its maturation.

One of the issues faced by start-up distillers of dark spirits is that it takes time for wood to impart its characteristics to the spirit. One technique is to use smaller barrels, which encourage the interaction needed between the wood and the whiskey—but Tuthilltown has another, less conventional trick. To agitate the barrels and encourage the spirit and the wood to interact, the warehouse is rigged up with a number of bass speakers. Dial up the volume, and sure enough the liquid in the barrels vibrates. Genius.

The proof of how good a job Tuthilltown is doing is in the tasting—and its entire range is highly awarded—but it's also evident in the ethos of everyone who's involved in the set-up. "It's pretty satisfying to say I ground the grain that made the whiskey that's in the bottle that you're pouring," says Ralph's son, Gable. And you can't argue with that. In 2014, William Grant & Sons, the family-owned Scottish distillers, took on Tuthilltown's Hudson brand for international distribution.

Tasting notes: There's a wise head on this young whiskey's shoulders, and it carries a sophisticated weight of spiced rye spliced with corn's sweetness. Butterscotch, toffee, and caramel notes are all there, toasty and correct. Tuthilltown are asking a premium price for this bad-boy—but there's such hit of aroma and flavor in the diminutive bottle that you can't help but feel this delivers.
Price: $$$$
Other products: Hudson Manhattan Rye Whiskey; Hudson New York Corn Whiskey; Hudson Single Malt Whiskey; Half Moon Orchard Gin; Tuthilltown Cassis Liqueur; Roggen's Rum; Indigenous Empire State Wheat Vodka
Web: tuthilltown.com

Hillrock Solera Aged Bourbon (46.3% abv)

HILLROCK ESTATE DISTILLERY, NEW YORK, USA

If bourbons were judged simply on their packaging (which, let's face it, many are), then Hillrock would be like rolling Brooks Brothers, Ralph Lauren, and L.L. Bean into one neat package. Its broad-shouldered bottle is crowned with a mahogany-colored wooden stopper and embellished and embossed with crests and monograms aplenty. The packaging isn't the only thing about this New York craft brand that tips the scales on the side of preppy.

Owned by real-estate-mogul turned gentleman farmer Jeffrey Baker, the distillery is set in a beautifully manicured estate in Ancram, which is topped off by a house dating from 1806 that was built by a Revolutionary War captain—not originally where it stands today, mind you, but some 161 km (100 miles) away on the shores of Lake George. Baker had the house dismantled and transported to his chosen site.

This may hint at a perfectionism that Baker carries over into his craft spirits brand—in order to develop Hillrock, he assembled a crack team around him, headed up by ex-Maker's Mark distiller Dave Pickerell, a formidable industry figure with 14 years' experience. Together with distiller Timothy Welly, former cellar master at Millbrook Winery, they have cultivated a grain-to-glass philosophy, growing the crops (selecting robust heirloom varieties), malting the barley (unusually, Baker decided to build a malthouse on site), and nurturing it through the distilling process.

Once the new-make spirit flows off the custom-built copper pot still, it goes through a rather unique aging process: Hillrock uses a Solera system, which is traditionally employed as a way to mature sherry, whereby barrels are only partially emptied before being topped up with new spirit (so there is always some of the oldest spirit mixing and mellowing in each barrel). It's finally "finished" by resting in 20-year-old Oloroso sherry casks, which adds a depth of flavor and complexity to the bourbon. The average age of the bourbon now coming out of the Solera is six years old.

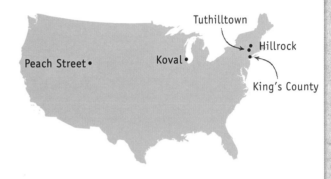

United States Bourbon Distilleries

Tuthilltown

Peach Street •

Koval •

Hillrock

King's County

Tasting notes: This is a lovely combination of warming, treacley molasses and spice (cloves and mulling spices), along with dried fruit and a top-note that touches on floral. Deep-flavored and delicious.
Price: $$$$$
Other products: Estate Rye and Estate Single Malt are coming soon...
Web: hillrockdistillery.com

King's County Distillery Bourbon (45% abv)

KINGS COUNTY DISTILLERY, BROOKLYN, USA

From the exposed brick walls of the century-old naval Paymaster building to the denim- and chunky-knit clad distillers David Haskell and Colin Spoelman, Kings County is the very picture of the urbane urban distillery. But the recent smattering of glossy book deals and photoshoots, which elevate these two above your standard garden-shed moonshine-makers, are evidence of a very recent success story that has its past in less photogenic (and less legal) roots.

Colin, who hails from Harlan—a "moist" county—had had his fair experience of drinking other people's moonshine before he began to experiment with his own. After a couple of years' apartment-based trial and error, Spoelman, along with partner David, decided that there was more to this than a cottage enterprise and, in 2010, they set themselves up in a diminutive loft in Williamsburg with five small stills and a big sense of ambition.

Production started on a limited scale. Using organic New York corn and a little malted barley from Scotland, the boys began to distil their own "moonshine"—essentially an unaged corn whiskey—along with a more serious bourbon, which they matured for at least 12 months. With packaging that many would've regarded as little more than sample bottles, the duo took their product to market and the reaction was good. More than good, in fact. Critics, bartenders, and punters lapped it up, and—when industry icon Jim Murray gave both whiskies starry ratings—anyone still to be convinced sat up and took notice.

With demand rapidly increasing, the Williamsburg site—possibly the tiniest distillery in the USA—quickly became impractically small, and so, in 2012, Haskell and Spoelman relocated to the old Navy Yard in Brooklyn. In doing so, they established the first New York City distillery to have operated (on the right side of the law) since Prohibition. Retro-fitting the building meant they could have it designed to their exacting specifications, and, along with the five small, stainless-steel stills, they set up Scottish-made gooseneck whiskey stills and NYC-crafted wooden fermenters made by Isseks Brothers. Nowadays, they even grow their own grain, with a corn and barley farm on site (how's that for racking up some serious locavore credentials?).

Along with myriad fans, industry accolades have also rolled in, and Kings County Distillery Moonshine and Bourbon have both been awarded ADI Craft Spirit Awards "best in category." These are spirits that effortlessly combine style with substance, made by two distillers who are—quite literally—poster boys for craft done brilliantly.

Tasting notes: Distilled from 70 percent New York corn and 30 percent malted barley, which is shipped in from Scotland, the whiskey is aged in small, new, American oak barrels. Perhaps it's the petite barrels, the level of char, or simply the liquid that they're filled with, but this is a spirit which belies its lack of years. Sophisticated notes of caramel, cinnamon, and cinder-toffee meld with the more lifted, corn-based sweetness to create a smooth and delicious drop. Kings County describes its ourbon as "precocious": they are quite right.
Price: $
Other products: Moonshine; Chocolate Whiskey
Web: kingscountydistillery.com

KINGS COUNTY DISTILLERY
bourbon whiskey
45% alcohol by volume, 375ml

Koval Single Barrel Bourbon (47% abv)

KOVAL DISTILLERY, CHICAGO, USA

To say that this impressively titled husband-and-wife team are invested in craft distilling is something of an understatement. Contrary to the straight-laced impression that their academic credentials might give, it was a feisty combination of entrepreneurial zeal and familial calling which prompted Dr. Robert Birnecker and Dr. Sonat Birnecker to fire up—you've guessed it—the first legal spirit stills in Chicago since Prohibition.

Austrian-born Robert has liquor (metaphorically) flowing in his veins, thanks to his spirit-producing grandparents. With hard-earned distilling qualifications and even harder-earned experience gained at the heels of various distilling maestro in Europe on his side, it may have been inevitable that he would one day return to his spirited roots. However, it wasn't until he and wife Sonat started toying with the idea of running a family business together that the dream of Koval Distillery was eventually conceived.

With an ambition to start craft distilling forged in 2008, when the movement was still in its infancy in the USA, Sonat and Robert invested everything they had in a (relatively small) 66-gallon (300-liter) still. Since then, the Birneckers have literally shaped the future of the micro-scene, advising well over a thousand small-scale producers in the USA and Canada about how to get started. (If their protégées are anywhere near as successful as Koval, then craft's future is in safe hands.)

Their expertise isn't simply in grain-to-glass distilling, though they sure as heck do that well, but also lies in the still technology—Sonat is the USA-based, English-speaking figurehead for Kothe Destillationstechnik, a German manufacturer which has supplied a vast number of USA start-ups.

Koval's own still is industry-leading, state-of-the-art kit: with sensors that continuously feed data and information to an iPad, and the ability to control certain of its capabilities remotely, Sonat and Robert believe there isn't a still to touch theirs in the USA. This example of German precision manufacturing at its finest means that Koval's distillers are able to get the cleanest, purest spirit cut.

But their bourbon is more than just a clean spirit: this, too, is industry-leading stuff. Along with organic, Midwestern-sourced corn, Sonat selected millet as the key other ingredient for the mash bill. Gluten-free and, they felt, a winning flavor counterpart to corn, this ancient grain adds balance and style to the spirit. Once distilled, it is matured in small, heavily charred barrels to help promote a heady, intensity of flavor, even in relative youth.

Tasting notes: Stewed apricots with cloves and star anise offer lush, sense-spiking overtures in the glass. Once tasted, a whisper of crème brûlée or crème pat lends angelic sweetness and cream on one side, while, on the other, you get a wallop of barbecue tastiness and peppery spice from the barrel char. Lip-smacking, gorgeous stuff.
Price: $$$
Other products: Koval Single Barrel Whiskey Four Grain; Koval Single Barrel Whiskey Millet; Koval Single Barrel Whiskey Oat; Koval Single Barrel Whiskey Rye; Koval Single Barrel White Whiskey Rye; Koval Apple Brandy; Koval Pear Brandy; Koval Bierbrand; Koval Sunchoke Spirit; Koval Vodka; and a range of fruit and floral liqueurs
Web: koval-distillery.com

Colorado Straight Bourbon (46% abv)

PEACH STREET DISTILLERS, COLORADO, USA

Among its plains and plateaus, canyons and rivers, Colorado can also boast 40 craft distilleries, the majority of which have sprung up, mushroom-like, in the past 12 months. However, Peach Street Distillers was (alongside Leopold Bros., see also *Vodka*, page 41) one of the founding fathers in the burgeoning scene. Located in Palisade, conveniently close to the soft fruit orchards, which ensure there's a good seasonal supply of local produce to turn into luscious liquor, PSD was established as the brainchild of Rory Donovan and Ska Brewing co-founders Dave Thibodeau and Bill Graham, along with head distiller Davy Lindig and the curiously named Moose Koons (apparently, he was a fat baby).

PSD's set-up means the fruit that it distils for its brands need never see the inside of a chiller trailer. Indeed, most of it is transported by forklift truck, with a maximum speed of 2 mph (3 km/h)—this really is a slow-food movement—and its grains all come from within a 5 mile (8 km) radius. This approach, Donovan explains, is central (and essential) to keeping their business sustainable, local, and appreciably craft.

Back in 2012, PSD was awarded "Distiller of the Year" by the American Distilling Institute, for which the audience of fellow distillers gave a standing ovation—these guys get the craft mentality, and their distilling colleagues fundamentally respect that. For example, when PSD says it small-batch distils, that's no mere marketing claim—even if they were to crank up their operation to 24 hours a day, they would still only run with a fraction of the capacity of much of their competition, producing around 1.3 barrels of bourbon a day. This small-scale process is, they reason, essential to transposing the unique, cereal-rich flavors of the local sweet corn to the spirit.

Once Peach Street's Bourbon has been aged in barrel in house, the distillery then reuses the wood to mature its single-malt whisky (rather than selling the barrels on to the second-hand market). And so, gloriously, the cycle of its spirit production turns on, bringing us more experimental, innovative, and crafted spirits.

Tasting notes: This neatly packaged bourbon showcases corn, both in the sweetness on the nose and the palate (where more rye-dominant bourbons would be tickling your throat with pepper). When it comes to mouthfeel and flavor, there's a lightness of touch (and a sense of its relative youth). However, its aromatic and fruity notes are thoroughly enjoyable, along with a sense of depth from the woody barrel char.

Price: $$$

Other products: Peach Brandy; Pear Brandy; Jackelope Gin; Jackelope & Jenny Gin; Eau de Vie; Grappa; D'Agave; Goat Artisan Vodka

Web: peachstreetdistillers.com

RYE

How much can popular culture influence us? What we eat and drink, how we dress, what we name our children? As the increasing number of Skylers and Khaleesis out there will, no doubt, attest: the answer is a *lot*. It should come as no surprise, then, that when television show *Mad Men* made its debut in 2007, managing to make workplace sexism and chain-smoking look pretty cool, the cocktail-swilling backdrop to life at Sterling Cooper would also slosh its way into our real-life drinking habits. Bartenders found that Old Fashioneds were suddenly back on the menu—and for real drinkers, that meant rye.

A WHISKEY WITH AN EDGE

Of course, the ryesurgence (sorry), which we've seen in recent years, shouldn't be wholly laid at the door of a television show: around a decade ago, spirit historians and geeks increasingly began to lament the forgotten charms of this spicy, all-American spirit in the press. Cocktails were invented for it! Wars were fought over it! Even Presidents distilled it! And yet, the spirit-drinking masses had been lured by the sweeter, smoother (or simply blander) charms of bourbon and vodka, and had left rye moldering in the dark. How could they? Well, quite simply because rye hasn't always tried very hard to be liked. It's no puppy-dog spirit; it isn't going to bound over and lick you in the face, and beg to be adored. No, it's the quirky, slightly oddball one—edgy, sometimes a bit sour, intense. You can imagine being cornered by it at a party.

While in the mid-Noughties, true mainstream demand may have been lacking, but enough momentum was building—coinciding beautifully with the budding craft movement in the USA—to inspire newbie distillers to rummage enthusiastically through drinking's archives, pull out old mash bills, and begin experimenting. The results were extremely encouraging: rye was hitting the spot with curious consumers and demand rocketed.

Today, rye is a hugely important category within the craft movement (and beyond); at its best, it shows exactly how vital craft can be, reinvigorating a forgotten alcohol style and proudly restoring it to its rightful place on the back bar. However, success can also bring strife: at the time of writing, "craft" rye has been in the press for "probably being made in a factory." This is because, in their haste to bring a product to market, some small-scale distillers have been tempted to skip the distil it/age it part of the process, going straight to the bottle it/flog it stage (tut tut). This is always going to be a danger area for start-ups, who want an aged product, but are too impatient to wait. As a result, their rush to market leaves a burgeoning sense of distrust in the authenticity of craft rye. For the buyer, this means careful research is key.

How rye is made

American rye whiskey is a very close relative of bourbon in terms of production (see *Bourbon*, pages 102–109). Its mash bill must contain at least 51 percent rye, with the rest usually made up of barley, wheat, and corn. As the characteristic tart, spicy sourness comes from the rye grain, many producers opt to make their product with a far higher proportion of rye in the mash to ensure it is distinct from other whiskey styles. Pennsylvania-style rye (also known as Monongahela-style) traditionally sport a mash bill of 100 percent rye.

Other rye-specific regulations state that it must be aged in new, charred-oak barrels; distilled to no more than 80% ABV; put into barrel for aging at no more than 62.5% ABV; and bottled at no less than 40%. Once the whiskey has been aged for at least two years, it may be called Straight Rye on the label.

It's worth pointing out that in Canada, whiskey is often called rye—a historical quirk that came about because its whiskey has often contained a proportion of rye grain in the mash bill. While the terms rye and whiskey are used interchangeably, it doesn't mean you'll be getting a rye-dominated dram, so keep an eye on the label.

Gunpowder Rye Whiskey (43.5% abv)

NEW ENGLAND DISTILLING, MAINE, USA

As a craft distiller just starting out, it's always going to be useful if you can point to a clutch of distilling-enthusiast relatives somewhere further up the family tree. For Ned Wight, who founded New England Distilling in Portland, Maine, in 2011, the family's distilling heritage must have felt like it was more than fate guiding him into the profession. His great-great-great-grandfather, John Jacob Wight, first took to the trade producing Sherwood Rye Whiskey in the 1850s, founding a family of distillers who would manage to survive Prohibition and continue distilling into the 1950s. In 1958, when the rye they were making just didn't match the tastes of the times, the stills finally ran dry.

Decades on, and some 500 miles (805 km) away from where his forebears were distilling, Ned is only too delighted to have brought Maryland-style rye back to the marketplace. "I grew up hearing about the family's distillery and how special Maryland rye whiskey was," he explains. "In fact, my father and I even threw around the idea of starting a distillery in the early Nineties with the thought of recreating the family's whiskies. What I don't believe in is legacy: while we make a Maryland-style rye whiskey, it's our own whiskey, not a recreation of some 'old family recipe.' We knew what Maryland rye tasted like and created our own interpretation of that style, incorporating the herbal character of old Maryland rye, along with some additional characteristics to create a whiskey that we love."

Ned came to the spirits industry via brewing (an interest he cultivated while at college, thanks to the encouragement of his room-mates), and—having seen the craft beer revolution—felt that the spirits movement was one he should be involved with.

"Distilling is one of those crafts that offers a unique meeting ground between history and technology, art and science," Ned says. And you can see this philosophy borne out in his distillery set-up, which has a bespoke, fire-heated copper pot still at its heart. He's also distinctly locavore in his approach to ingredients, sourcing Maine grain and using a yeast from Maine Beer Company's Mean Old Tom and Zoe to ferment his washes.

In order to establish a cash flow for the distillery, Ned's first project was to release his Ingenium Gin. Meanwhile, his Maryland rye was gently maturing in new-oak barrels (resting, rather poetically, on racks he managed to salvage from the old Sherwood distillery). Eschewing corn in favor of barley, the mash bill for Ned's Maryland style of rye is both spicy and herbaceous with no concession made to the sweetness that corn can bring ("What we're looking for is the right balance of the rye spice and herbal character with the caramel, toast, and vanilla character from the barrel," he says). "While I was still in the very early dream phases of starting the distillery, rye was not a product that was being consumed in any notable quantity in the USA. What rye folks were drinking was a Midwestern style, not Maryland rye. I had this vision of being a part of the re-introduction of a wonderful, old, and largely forgotten style of American whiskey." Bringing it to market in November 2013 must have felt like history coming full circle—only this time, it's exactly suited to the tastes of the time, and critics and consumers love it.

Tasting notes: While the nose promises power and spice and all things nice, the palate delivers a pungent, peppery spirit with a lick of really bitter chocolate and some vanilla woodiness.
Price: $$
Other products: Ingenium Gin; Eight Bells Rum
Web: newenglanddistilling.com

Ryemageddon (46% abv) CORSAIR, NASHVILLE, USA

Unconventional, experimental, and deliberately in-yer-face, Corsair is a craft distillery with attitude. The idea to distil came about when friends Darek Bell and Andrew Webber, who were already united in their penchant for home-brewing, got distracted from a bio-fuels project which they were working on with the idea that making whiskey would be a whole lot more rewarding. Turns out, that hunch was right, and they are now one of the most awarded (and respected) craft distilleries on the block.

Corsair operates two sites and has two stills, one is an antique 250-gallon (1,137-liter), pre-Prohibition gin still, which is used to make some of their more straightforward products, and the other (sited in Bowling Green, Kentucky) is a tricked-up, 50-gallon (227-liter) pot still that Darek and Andrew commissioned from Vendome. It's designed to be "the Batmobile" of distilling, as, although it only caters for tiny batches of spirit production, it can do whatever you need it to do. With bubble plates and a Carter-head capacity, it can either be used to take ultra-precise cuts of spirit to isolate a particular flavor or to infuse a spirit with spices or botanicals. Its versatility is undoubtedly responsible for some of the more outré productions seen so far, a non-exhaustive list of which follows.

While the distillery came to market—and attention—with its gin and absinthe, there's no doubting where the real passion lies: whiskey, for which the distillers are messing around with different kinds of grain (ancient and modern), mash bills, smoke, wood, and so on. "Creativity is free," Darek is quick to point out—not only that, but it also means that there's a whopping point of difference between them and the big boys with the mega marketing budgets.

Tasting notes: This is double distilled, first in the big still, then in the small-batch one to allow the boys to take the cut with just the right amount of spice, pepper, and "the cereal taste of rye which we love," they say. The mash bill is 80 percent rye, with the remaining 20 percent coming from chocolate rye. Its nose is sneezingly peppery with spice too; on the palate, this is a racy, dark mouthful with gorgeous, sour-rye-bread complexity.

Price: $$$

Other products: Cherrywood Smoke American Malt Whiskey; Citra Double IPA American Malt Whiskey; Elderflower Bohemian American Malt Whiskey; Grainiac Tennessee Bourbon; Hop Monster American Whiskey; Insane in the Grain 12-Grain Bourbon; Nashville Tennessee Bourbon; Oak Smoked Wheat Whiskey; Oatmeal Stout American Whiskey; Old Punk Whiskey; Quinoa Whiskey; Rasputin American Malt Whiskey; Triple Smoke American Malt Whiskey; Triticale Whiskey; Wry Moon Unaged Kentucky Whiskey; Artisan Gin; Spiced Rum; Vanilla Bean Vodka; Pumpkin Spice Moonshine; Red Absinthe

Web: corsairartisan.com

Dark Horse •

• Corsair

• New England

US Rye Distilleries

Dark Horse Distillery Reunion Rye Whiskey (44.5% abv)

DARK HORSE DISTILLERY, KANSAS, USA

If the only thing you love more than your "better half" is a good liquor tour, then happy news: you can now tie the knot in this Kansas-based distillery. (If, though, it's rather too far from home, then at least Dark Horse's gold-medal-winning bourbon and whiskies are also easy to fall for.)

Patrick, Damian, Eric, and Mary Garcia, the siblings behind DHD, knew they wanted to set up a family business, but were unsure which direction to take. "We saw the craft distilling movement coming through the country, so we started touring distilleries to feel the pulse of the industry," says Patrick Garcia. Duly inspired, Patrick began to educate himself in the mechanics of distilling and in 2010 the Dark Horse Distillery took a "leap of faith" and broke ground. By May 2011, construction was complete and their bespoke still—affectionately known as Chester Copperpot (very cute) and made by copper-workers Vendome—was in place and beginning to do its thing. Ten 500-gallon (2,273-liter) fermenters were another clear sign that these guys were seriously in business.

"We bring the grain in, mill it, mash it, and ferment it, and then distil it," says Patrick, who is the master distiller at Dark Horse, emphasizing that their process is totally grain to glass. "Everything is small-batch, so we are able to make a cut that puts the heart into the barrel," he explains. The tighter the cut, the better the spirit, and Patrick takes around 10 percent on his primary distillation.

The first batches of Dark Horse bourbon and rye were cooked up in June 2011, before being safely stowed in micro-barrels, which are an extremely significant ingredient. Small-scale and specially commissioned, they were made from Missouri oak and designed with an internal honeycomb pattern to encourage plenty of contact with wood (the more interaction there is between wood and spirit, the faster the liquor will mature.) It proved a smart move: the Garcias' choice of barrels meant that they were able to launch their finished rye and bourbon in 2013, both of which show a sophistication and maturity that belie their brief years.

Of course, for a craft distiller, two years is a long time to sit without an income, so while DHD's bourbon and rye were busily maturing, two unaged products—a vodka and a white whiskey—were launched to ensure that there was the requisite cash flow coming in to the distillery. Whether aged or not, the Garcias practice a craft process right up to the finish line. All of Dark Horse's spirits are hand-bottled, hand-labeled, and individually numbered. "There's a lot of hard work that goes on here, but we love it," says Patrick.

Tasting notes: Made from a mash bill that's an unapologetic 100 percent rye, this old-style whiskey gives serious spice on the nose, along with a characteristically sour-rye-bread twang. On the palate, there is real caramel and toffee, loads of cracked black pepper, spice, and a pleasant, lingering finish.
Price: $$
Other products: Dark Horse Distillery Reserve Bourbon Whiskey; Long Shot White Whiskey; Rider Vodka
Web: dhdistillery.com

WHITE WHISKEY AND WHITE DOG

What is it with white whiskey? The mere mention of the stuff is enough to make a Scotsman choke on his single malt, and yet, across the USA (and increasingly globally), there is a tribe of evangelists proclaiming the unadulterated glories of what is essentially new-make spirit bottled in the same condition as it flows off the still.

AN ALTERNATIVE HAIR OF THE DOG

Also known as white dog, this isn't simply a distilling phenomenon of the craft classes. The big players—Jim Beam and Diageo, for example—have all enthusiastically weighed into the market. And who can blame them? With a fortune saved on wood and warehousing, not to mention the massive financial advantage of being able to make a spirit and then sell it on immediately (especially when the supply of older stocks is becoming an issue for the industry), white whiskey is a category where everyone is a winner. Or are they?

What's in a name?

Before we launch ourselves too enthusiastically onto the bandwagon, it's worth pausing to consider why that self-same Scotsman would go all William Wallace on you at the mere mention of a white whiskey. In Scotland, where the industry is tightly quality-controlled, a spirit must be aged for three years and a day before it can carry the term "whisky." This isn't for spurious reasons of history or heritage, but rather because the wood has such an important role to play in a spirit—it gives it color, obviously, but also a great deal of the flavor (up to 70 percent, some would argue) stems from the spirit's interaction with the barrel.

Here, the argument comes full circle: without the wood, you get a sensational, purist's experience—spirit in its unadulterated form. Bartenders love it for cocktails; spirits geeks love it for exploring real nuances of flavor. And, however you cut it, this is exciting stuff: in the craft market, we're not talking about rough-as-boots moonshine but, instead, a flavorful, characterful, punchy spirit which needs to be tasted so that you can fully appreciate the might of white.

Vit Hund (46.1% abv)

MACKMYRA, GÄVLE, SWEDEN

Before we delve into the story behind Sweden's first whiskey distillery, consider its artisan distilling processes, or its numerous awards, we should take a moment to appreciate the more superficial matter of its Vit Hund packaging. The bottle itself is sleek enough, but the clever bit is the brown paper bag wrapping, stamped with a white dog logo. It's knowing, it's funny, and it looks cool. Good job.

Now to what lies beneath. Back in 1998—a lifetime in craft distilling years—a group of friends on a skiing holiday (naturally, this is Sweden) were, while indulging in a selection of different whiskies, lamenting the fact that there wasn't a Swedish single malt to bring to the table. A year later, on December 18, 1999, those same eight whiskey-loving friends were gathered around their own still as the first drops of Mackmyra flowed.

These guys have gone to great lengths to create whiskey that demonstrates real *terroir*, from the sourcing of the grain—which is traceable right down to the exact field where the barley is grown—through to the culmination of the process: maturation in carefully selected Swedish oak barrels (petite 6.5-gallon/30-liter casks). Should you venture further into the range to taste beyond the Vit Hund (which you surely should), you can discern the impact of this rarely used wood, along with some pretty sensational smoke.

Mackmyra creates its smoky flavors by adapting the traditional peated whiskey process: peat is cut from the nearby peat bog "Karinmossen," before being seasoned with fresh juniper wood to impart a unique spice and flavour. The grains are then smoked so they can absorb these unique and wonderful flavors.

The unsmoked Vit Hund, however, is the place for purists to begin their introduction to the brand, tasting as you can the spirit in its raw, unadulterated form.

Tasting notes: Bottled at a punchy 46%, you would expect something of a wallop of alcohol on the nose but, instead, are met with a pleasant, citrusy, and lightly floral nose. The palate has cereal sweetness, and you get more barley/hay/grassiness, which winds itself up to a finish that warms rather than burns.
Price: $$$
Other products: Mackmyra Brukswhisky; Mackmyra Special; Svensk Rök; Bee (a honey liqueur)
Web: mackmyra.com

Swedish White Whiskey Distilleries

Mackmyra

Death's Door White Whisky (40% abv)

DEATH'S DOOR SPIRITS, WISCONSIN, USA

The rather gothic-sounding Death's Door Spirits company arose, not out of the wild obsession of a band of liquor geeks, but rather through the more earthy concern of whether a farming community could be revived on Washington Island. Initially, 5 acres (2 hectares) of the agricultural land was planted by brothers Tom and Ken Koyen to produce enough wheat to supply a start-up brewery called Capital. The venture was a success and, gradually, an increasing number of farmers saw their way back into what had become a redundant profession. To meet the demand from Capital Brewers, and now Death's Door Spirits, more than a 1,000 acres (400 hectares) have been planted with hard red winter wheat (a grain found to be uniquely well-suited to the maritime climate).

From these rather noble roots has sprung a serious craft spirits company, headed by founder (and for a number of years sole employee) Brian Ellison. Ellison's background is in land management rather than distilling; he saw the idea of a spirits company as the logical next step after the Capital craft brewery. He named the distillery Death's Door after the— notoriously lethal—passage of water that separates Washington Island from Wisconsin (at least 350 wrecks languish at the bottom of the ocean there), which has to be navigated by the boats carrying the grain to the Wisconsin-based distillery.

Now, aided and abetted by John Jeffery, the head of distilling, and John Kinder, who leads the branding side of things, Death's Door has grown in scale and product range, which now includes a gin, a vodka, and an excellent white whiskey.

To produce the whiskey, a mash bill of 80 percent Washington Island wheat is married with Wisconsin malted barley to create a low-alcohol beer which is then double distilled before being "rested" in stainless-steel vats. Although it is resolutely unaged, it does spend a fleeting amount of time—a mere 72-hour mini-break—being finished in virgin oak barrels from Minnesota, which results in a smooth, clear spirit (made in a way that leaves you with an even clearer conscious).

US Whiskey Distilleries

Death's Door •

→ FEW

Tasting notes: On the nose, along with grainy spice, there is a whiff of something pleasantly herbaceous (dried-herb bouquet garni), along with an asparagus-like vegetal note that trundles along into the more familiar territory of marzipan/cherry-stone sweetness and spicy, zesty kick.
Price: $$
Other products: Death's Door Gin; Death's Door Vodka
Web: deathsdoorspirits.com

nb: The bottle shown here is the UK version, the US bottle has a slightly different label

FEW White Whiskey (40% abv)

FEW SPIRITS, CHICAGO, USA

While there are legions of craft distillers in the USA that declare they are "the first operational distillery in [insert town name here] since Prohibition," FEW has a deliciously appealing Prohibition-related claim. It takes its name from the initials of Frances Elizabeth Willard, a woman who was at the forefront of the temperance league and who made her base in Evanston, just outside Chicago—precisely where Paul Hletko has established his distillery.

With alcohol in his bloodline (his Czech grandfather was a brewer), Hletko saw the town's ultra-dry status as more of a challenge than an obstacle. He successfully campaigned for the law to be changed to legitimize micro-distillers—a process which took about a year— before the stills could finally swing into operation in June 2011.

Two copper pots form the backbone of the distillery, one of which—a bespoke German model—is dedicated to whiskey production, while the other is required for its (excellent) gin. Its white whiskey— a double-gold award winner, which marks it out for particular attention—is made from a mash bill of mainly corn (70 percent), with the remainder coming from wheat and malted barley.

Tasting notes: Those worried that a whiff of white whiskey will be enough to anesthetize their nasal passages need have no such concern with this sweetly approachable white whiskey. There's undoubtedly corn on the nose, followed by peppery spice, and then on the palate an almost a marzipan, cherry-stone dash of complexity before its warming sign-off. A bit of rough this is not.

Price: $$$

Other products: FEW Bourbon Whiskey; FEW Rye Whiskey; FEW American Gin; and occasional special releases

Web: fewspirits.com

POITÍN

The Irish spirit poitín (sometimes spelled poteen or potcheen, the latter being—roughly—how it's pronounced) has a history that spans hundreds of years, occupies both sides of the law, and involves old-school, wily, innovative, and rogueish characters, along with much more sensible modern craft spirit distillers. Defining exactly what the spirit is is tricky—through the ages no one has really recorded its recipe, far less made rules about what can and can't go into the still—but, roughly speaking, we are talking about a pot-distilled white whiskey, unaged, and eye-wateringly (no, make that blindingly) strong, which is now protected by EU-controlled geographical status.

OVER 500 YEARS IN THE MAKING

Poitín distilling was a largely rural practice, whereby surplus crops were fermented into a beer before being pot-distilled. Barley was the traditional base for poitín but, over the years, molasses, sugar beet, potatoes (and, doubtless, any surplus fruit or cereal) have all been used in the mix. In old-school poitín-making, the barley would first be steeped in a bog hole or river, along with a measure of oats, for a day and a night before being drained. Once the excess water was removed, the grains soon began to germinate; they were spread over a floor to encourage this process and keep air circulating. The grains would be turned every evening for a week to get a good, even germination. On the eighth day, the barley and oats would be kiln-heated and dried to halt germination. Throughout Connemara, on Ireland's West Coast, turf-covered, stone-built kilns are still set into the hillsides.

Producing the spirit provided a handy revenue stream for local farmers who had big rent bills to meet, and was a way of life for most communities. This all changed on Christmas Day 1661, when the English introduced a hefty taxation on alcohol. Overnight, poitín-making became as much about the art of subterfuge as it was about distilling. Just over a hundred years later, it became illegal to run a home-still without a licence, confirming poitín's outlawed, Robin Hood status.

Where, previously, stills could be visibly located in outbuildings or on farmers' land, once the Revenue was on the trail of distillers, a great deal more discretion and nouce was required. Those intending to distil would site their temporary pot stills on land boundaries, so that ownership could be disputed if necessary, or on common ground so that those involved could scarper at the first sign of the law. The upshot of this opportunistic distilling was that the stills could be quickly assembled and were very simple. Joints were sealed with a paste made from oatmeal, prior to the stills being lit, to prevent any leakage, and the stills were fired with only the driest turf, so that minimal smoke was visible from the distilling site.

These pop-up stills could handle a barrel of fermented barley beer at any one time. Using this quantity of liquid, it took around four hours to produce a batch of "singling," which would comprise around 4 gallons (18 liters) or so of new-make spirit. As the spirit trickled off, the first part—the fusel oils—were gathered and dumped. Next came the "heart" of the spirit, which was carefully collected. As the "heart" was coming to an end, the distiller would use a highly scientific method (i.e. attempting to set light to it) to make sure that only the "best" alcohols were still coming through. Once the liquid no longer lit easily, the distiller would pronounce that the "feints" had arrived and the distillation was finished. (Terrifyingly, the feints were then, apparently, set apart to be used for medicine…). The final step in the poitín-making process was to re-distil the singling to produce the "doubling"—the new-make spirit that would be bottled at anywhere up to 90% proof. Yes, that's right, 90.

Having spent roughly 500 years being enthusiastically produced on the wrong side of the law, in 1997 United Distillers (owned by Guinness) announced that it was to produce a poitín and the spirit began its journey back toward the mainstream. In July 2007, the EU formally gave it geographically protected status, which, chiming nicely with the rise of craft in Europe, gave a new wave of distillers the impetus to create their own versions of this fabled spirit.

Gather up the pots and the old tin can
And the mash, and the corn, the barley,
and the bran
And then run like the devil from the excise man
Keep the smoke from rising, Barney.

"Hills Of Connemara" (Sean McCarthy)

Glendalough Mountain Strength Poitin (60% abv)

GLENDALOUGH IRISH WHISKEY COMPANY, WICKLOW, IRELAND

Five bearded friends from Dublin and Wicklow, along with a pretty exciting celebrity backer in the form of former Irish rugby pro Brian O'Driscoll, are the backbone of this textbook craft start-up.

Established in 2011 (the boys claim theirs to be Ireland's "first craft distillery"—this can only be true if we consider distillers of the modern generation), Glendalough, which is just now poised to release its first whiskey, launched itself onto the market in 2013 with a trio of superbly exciting poitíns and the ambitious aim to bring Irish distilling back to its traditional roots.

Although the Glendalough distillery is now distilling in its own right, the first products the boys brought to market were made under licence by West Cork Distillers. The mash bill combines malted barley with Irish sugar beet, which is fermented for 72 hours before being distilled. Dónal Ó'Gallachóir, the brand manager for Glendalough says: "After it is carefully batch-distilled, it's matured in Irish oak for up to six months. This allows the spirit to interact with the wood, mellow and smooth out, and to gain more flavor."

Irish Poitín Distilleries

Teeling

Glendalough •

Tasting notes: The alcohol on the nose is a tickle rather than a slap, which is surprising considering the potency of this particular poitín. Cracked black pepper and spice are far more abundant at this strength (rather than the Premium version), so it's worth opting for the 60% and adding your preferred water to taste. The virgin wood doesn't contribute flavor, but may be responsible for the poitín's undeniable smoothness. This is not for the faint of heart mind you.
Price: $$$
Other products: Glendalough 7-Year-Old Single Malt; Glendalough Premium Poitín; Glendalough Sherry Cask Finish Poitín; Glendalough Summer Gin
Web: glendaloughdistillery.com

The Teeling Whiskey Company Poitin (61.5% abv)

TEELING WHISKEY COMPANY, DUBLIN, IRELAND

Coming, as they do, from an old whiskey family, Jack and Steve Teeling know a thing or two about spirits. When Cooley Distillery, one of the only independents in Ireland, which was established by their father in the Eighties, was sold in 2012 to Illinois-based behemoth Beam, the boys decided that this was the cue they needed to go out and set up on their own.

Tapping into their history, a look into the archives revealed that the brothers' forebear Walter Teeling first distilled in Dublin itself, in The Liberties, back in the late-18th century, when there was something of a golden age for spirits in the city. Reviving this tradition seemed a pretty noble aspiration, and so Jack and Steve set about the bureaucratic battle, and the multi-million Euro investment, required to move a distillery back into the self-same part of town. The end of the red tape has just about come into sight, and the first distillery to open in Dublin in 125 years is underway.

So, here comes an important disclaimer: those spirits that are currently released under the Teeling label haven't been produced in their own stills (in fact, Jack predicts that these won't be on the shelves until 2018), but, instead, have been selected, blended, and finished by the boys, who have drawn on every industry contact and knocked on just about every door in Irish whiskey to ensure they have good-enough historic stocks to work with. For their new-make spirit, they have gone to their old distillery, Cooley.

Poitín, of course, is unaged white whiskey, straight off the still. Jack decided that they wanted to include it in the Teeling range, as it remains such an integral part of Irish drinking culture. "Even to this day, if you go to a celebration—whether a wake or a wedding—there'll always be someone with a bottle of 'the queer stuff,' as they call it down the country. It's still very much a craft that's practiced, albeit illicitly," he says. "We see poitín as the original spirit of Ireland—we wanted to try to drag it out of the shadows and present it in a way that would appeal to a new generation of drinkers in Ireland and around the world. Being inspired by what has happened in the USA with moonshine and white dog, we wanted to make this because it's also interesting for whiskey drinkers to try an unaged Irish spirit that, if put in wood, would become Irish whiskey.

"Our mash bill consists of new-make malt spirit, but also some new-make grain spirit. The combination of both produces a flavorsome but smooth spirit that is very drinkable in its own right." Teeling's may not be quite the 100 percent, pot-distilled poitín that traditionalists might advocate, but, for the uninitiated, it's a good place to start.

Tasting notes: Don't be lulled into a false sense of security by the almost sugary/bubble-gum nose: neither the sweetness nor the candy-shop associations follow through onto the palate, which sits somewhere between the comforting flavors of dough and a wallop of alcohol and warming citrus/spice, along with those sugared almonds that come in favor bags at weddings. You'll need to cut it with water to really savor it (without needing an early bath) and, when you do so, there's a creamy mouthfeel that comes through, too. Interesting stuff.

Price: $$

Other products: Teeling Small Batch; Teeling Small Grain; Teeling Vintage Reserve 21

Web: teelingwhiskey.com

BRANDY

When we think of brandy, we tend to think of a spirit made from wine—a fine Cognac, perhaps, to which you need only add a cigar, a fireside armchair, and a diminutive château in order to truly appreciate its subtleties. But brandies don't need to come from a specific region of France, nor are they limited to grape juice as their raw material (any fermented fruit can, technically, be turned into a brandy, as long as the label refers to the product as "fruit brandy"). For the sake of clarity, this section has been split into brandy (wine-based) and fruit brandies (which are more "go nuts and distil what you like" kind of products). You can guess which is more suited to the modern craft distiller. Whether grape-based or made from other fruit, all new-make spirit must be aged for two years in wood in order to carry the term "brandy."

BRANDY (THE WINE KIND)

Brandy is made throughout the world wherever grapes can be grown. The wines used to make it, however, would barely be palatable if drunk pre-distillation, as they are highly acidic and relatively low-alcohol (these characteristics tend to create the best spirit). Although France chalks up the two most famous appellations (the aforementioned Cognac, the brandies of which the French export, and Armagnac, the brandies of which the French drink), Spain, Mexico, and South Africa are also big producers, while in Chile and Peru brandy is usually unaged, aromatic, and referred to as pisco.

While it's as well to be aware of the world's most famous brandy region, Cognac, for our purposes, it can hardly be considered the heartland of a modern craft movement—rather, the region's very established trade tends to supply a sophisticated export market (mainly in the USA and UK) and is dominated by a few extremely historic distillers, some of which are owned by multinational drinks companies and large commercial players. The spirit's high-profile celebrity customers, its popularity as a statement luxury gift, and the flow of ever-more-eye-wateringly expensive special releases increasingly raise the eyebrows of "serious" drinkers. Meanwhile, for the French, Cognac continues to be dismissed as lacking in complexity and depth when compared with the more robust and challenging world of Armagnac (which is currently enjoying rapid gains in popularity beyond Gallic shores).

The marked difference in flavor profiles between France's two acclaimed spirits is in large part thanks to their distinct distillation processes. Where, in Cognac, law dictates that a Charentais pot still must be used, in Armagnac—where the art of distillation was learned from Spain's Moorish occupants—Alambic Armagnacais distillation is the most common practice. Since we will find the two different styles of distilling put into play throughout the brandy-making world, it's as well to understand how and why they make different liquors.

The Charentais still

Cognac must be double distilled in a Charentais copper pot still, which all follow the same basic design and so are not credited with imparting much character to the spirit—that comes, instead, from the character of the wine and the aging process. The still combines a heat source/furnace, a small pot with a still head (shaped like a garlic bulb), and a swan's neck that narrows and twists into a coil, which is housed in a condensing unit. The wine is often pre-warmed before it goes into the pot to save energy. During the second distillation (which is known as *la bonne chauffe*), the distiller will separate the heads and tails, while the heart goes on to be matured. The cut is usually of good quality and relatively congener-light.

The Alambic Armagnacais still

The majority of Armagnac is distilled only once, leaving behind far more "flavor" (or "impurities," depending on which side of the Armagnac versus Cognac debate you fall). The set-up here is basically that of a column still, albeit with far fewer rectification plates than would be used to distil, say, vodka. Picture two columns, one sitting on a heat source, the other over a receiving vessel, with each joined to the other by pipes at the top. The column over the heat source has around seven rectification plates in it; the column over the receiving vessel has a condensing coil running down it. Wine flows into the top of the heated column, where it passes up through the plates, evaporates, and travels as vapor across into the condensing coil from where it's collected. These stills are usually run at quite a high temperature, and this—plus the fact the spirit goes through few plates and is distilled only once—can result in the production of quite a raw or rough-tasting liquor. This means that

the aging process is critical to the success of Armagnac. Such is the small scale (and rural nature) of a lot of Armagnac production that much of it is made by mobile distillers (see *Fruit Brandies*, pages 136–139, for more on these).

Brandy producers

Scandalously, we are now going to virtually ignore the fine brandies of both Cognac and Armagnac, as neither has a place here: you have probably been drinking your favorite brand of the former for years. The latter (by and large) is produced by hundreds of very, very small-scale farmers, many of whom don't release what they make commercially, rendering descriptions either of the producers or their products redundant. However, if you are yet to taste Armagnac, then one brand that you may be lucky enough to happen upon is Chateau de Tariquet, the background of which is a glorious tale of love, war, and triumph in the face of adversity, which is too good to gloss over.

Château du Tariquet Classique VS (40% abv)

CHÂTEAU DU TARIQUET, BAS-ARMAGNAC, FRANCE

This story begins, as the best ones should, with bears. In late-19th-century France, living in the foothills of the Pyrenees in the village of Ercé, was a bear-tamer of some repute named Artaud. Artaud was a young man who sought adventure, and so, with two of his bears in tow, he made the epic sea journey to America. There, he lived and loved and had a son, Jean Pierre, who married a Frenchwoman named Pauline. In his dotage, Artaud felt the pull of his motherland, and returned home in 1912. There, in the heart of the Bas-Armagnac region, he came across the Tariquet estate, which had been brought to its knees post-phylloxera (a virus that decimated French vineyards in the 19th century). Despite its disrepair, Artaud saw the future of his family writ large, and, along with investment from his son, bought it.

Jean Pierre had remained in New York with his bride, but the outbreak of war in 1914 saw him return to France to do his patriotic duty. He sustained a bayonette wound in combat that was to render him all but unrecognizable: Pauline, who met each of the hospital ships that brought the injured from Le Havre to New York, was eventually rewarded when he returned to her in 1922. The world had changed, and Pauline and Jean Pierre moved back to France where they had a daughter, Hélène.

Some years later, following the outbreak of the Second World War, Hélène was to meet a dashing resistance fighter, Pierre Grassa. The two fell madly in love and—along with the four children that would come from their marriage—set about nurturing Tariquet back to its pre-war glories and ensured that the family-owned estate had a great future ahead of it.

Today, with 2,224 acres (900 hectares) of land planted to grapes for their own wine and Armagnac production, they run a 100 percent vineyard-to-bottle operation. The minority of the estate is planted to Armagnac grapes, but here their choices have been sophisticated: including the notoriously diva-ish Folle Blanche and the unusual Plante De Graisse. Harvest takes place in the fall (autumn), the exact date depending on that vintage's conditions, and the grapes are pressed and fermented. Once the first frosts arrive, it's time for the annual distillation season to begin, which is kicked off with a big family feast. The wood-fire-heated Armagnac still is run for 10-day stretches until the wine yield has been exhausted and the spirit begins its journey through the barrels for aging.

Eventually, the aged spirits are blended and allowed time to marry; the Armagnac is then bottled by hand.

Tasting notes: Distilled from a blend of Ugni Blanc and Baco grapes, this—the youngest of the aged Armagnacs in the stable—has wonderful, oak-driven vanilla, elegant floral notes, and a stewed-fruit (prunes) richness and complexity.
Price: $$
Other products: Armagnac Cabine; Blanche AOC; Château du Tariquet Hors d'Âge; Château du Tariquet VSOP; Château du Tariquet XO; Le Légendaire; 1995; 1994; 1993; 1988
Web: tariquet.com

French Brandy Distilleries

• Château du Tariquet

Copper & Kings Immature Brandy (45% abv)

COPPER & KINGS AMERICAN CRAFT BRANDY, KENTUCKY, USA

Butchertown, Louisville, Kentucky—heartland of bourbon production—is home to some new kids on the block in the distilling world, and (unusually) they're making brandy. Having started production in spring 2014, the factory-fresh stills are gleaming and everything in the distillery is new-make (not just the spirits). Joe and Lesley Heron, who having recently sold their existing drinks companies Nutrisoda and Crispin Cider to the (distinctly un-craft) PepsiAmericas and MillerCoors, decided to embark on a project that they could build from the ground up.

"Lesley and I are interested in starting beverage businesses that operate in the space that will become cool next, not now. Brandy appears to us to be in that space," says Joe. "Brandy is an original American spirit, yet over the years has fallen from the US lexicon and been replaced by bourbon. We have an aspiration to return brandy to the portfolio of fine American spirits."

Their traditionally shaped, beautifully made stills come from near neighbor Vendome. Joe and Lesley were able to collaborate on a specially customized design that, though based on a Charantais shape, was unique to them, ensuring maximum spirit contact with the copper to produce a spirit that was both clean and characterful. The "reducing elbow" in the swan's neck encourages reflux, and they twice-distil for greater purity in their spirit.

Wood-wise, Copper & Kings couldn't be located in a better place, with its pick of both coopers and ex-bourbon barrels right on the distillery doorstep. At the time of writing, their new-make spirit was beginning its two-year journey to maturation (with admirable, but uncommon, transparency C&K have released a Craft Brandy that, although blended by them, was made by "some outstanding distillers kind enough to share their aged stock.") Though this might have a soupçon of the company's DNA in it showing through the blend, for a real taste of what's to come you need to look to the Immature Brandy, distilled from a Muscat-based wine sourced from California.

"We are also distilling Kentucky Vidal Blanc wine (Vidal Blanc being a hybrid between Ugni Blanc and Seyval Blanc); we have experimented with both Norton and Concord varietals," says Joe. "We also have a spectacular Apple Brandy coming up and will be launching our Absinthe Blanche soon. This is a classic absinthe using classic absinthe botanicals distilled with a Muscat base. Our imaginations have not stopped—we have an extensive barrel-aging program that includes: absinthe aged in juniper, bourbon, port, and rye barrels, as well as gin aged in juniper barrels (we have used an apple brandy base for our gin). And we are just getting started. There's a lot more in the pipeline."

Tasting notes: Pear drops and grape juice, grass and light floral notes combine. With gentle alcohol and youthful charm, this hints at good things still to come.
Price: $
Other products: Copper & Kings Craft Distilled Brandy
Web: copperandkings.com

US Brandy Distilleries

• Germain-Robin   Copper & Kings •

Harvest Spirits

Craft Method Brandy (40% abv)

GERMAIN-ROBIN, CALIFORNIA, USA

When a spirit has been repeatedly dubbed "the best on the planet," it's bound to garner attention; when that self-same spirit is the product of the very beginning of America's craft spirit movement, then it's time to get even more excited. More than 30 years ago, when St. George (see *Gin*, page 60, and *Absinthe*, page 142) was setting up in San Francisco, Mendocino County was seeing its own piece of distilling history being made.

Germain-Robin started with a truly chance encounter: Ansley Coale happened to pick up a hitchhiker, Hubert Germain-Robin, on Highway 101. Telling his story, as travelers often do, Hubert relayed the tale of his family's centuries-old Cognac distillery, of its sale to a large conglomerate, and his disappointment in the state of the industry. The seed of an idea was planted and Ansely, fascinated as he was by the old-world appeal of distilling, proposed that they set up a small-scale, hand-run operation right there in California.

Hubert sourced and shipped in an old Cognac still; a shed was duly built, and they began the quest to find the right grapes. Located as it was in prime wine country, there was no shortage of superb fruit to be had. While Cognac is traditionally distilled from acidic, unpalatable wine, with the pick of the vineyards at their disposal for relatively little money, the pair began to experiment with different varieties that nobody had distilled before. "It took years to get it right—there was nobody we could go to," says Ansley. "Each of the varietals needs to be distilled in its own way." However, a Pinot Noir produced a spirit that was—according to Hubert—the finest he had experienced. Today, an old-vine Semillon from a 5-acre (2-hectare) plot in the McDonald valley is the source of some of their favorite grapes: this particular fruit produces "a rich, deep brandy that gives a lot of volume in the mouth, but which ages slowly."

It's not just the base wine that is critical: how the still is run is also an art, and each distillation needs to be nursed and assessed individually to get the best from that particular wine. The temperature of the still can be adjusted to highlight characteristics that the distiller wants to enhance, or to minimize something funky which doesn't sit right in the brandy.

Aging is, says Ansely, where 80 percent of the work happens, and it's crucial to have knowledge of what's in each of the barrels and how the spirit is maturing. The barrels they use are $1,000 each, made from Limousin oak by a French craftsman ("he's one of the last guys who air-dries his oak")— essential, Ansely explains, to retain the delicate and fruity character of the style of brandy they produce.

Tasting notes: Easily compared with a fine Cognac, this has a rich, warm, and inviting nose with floral lift and baked fruit. To taste, the succulent mouthfeel is immediately striking, with a gorgeously smooth texture and length, and a lovely crème anglaise, orchard-fruit sweetness and vanilla on the finish. Pure class.
Price: $$$
Other products: Anno Domini; Coast Road Reserve; Heirloom Apple Brandy; Old Havana Brandy; Select Barrel XO; Single Barrel Varietal Brandies; Small Blends; Varietal Grappa
Web: germain-robin.com

Savingnac Potstill Brandy (40% abv)

JORGENSEN'S, WELLINGTON, SOUTH AFRICA

It's little surprise that South Africa's Western Cape—home to some of the world's best wineries—is also home to some of the world's most delicious, grape-based brandy. In fact, such is the number of distilleries in the area that brandy tourism is a popular pastime, although few distilleries have embraced the craft mentality quite like Jorgensen's.

A farmer by profession, Roger first turned his hand to distillation in 1994, creating the set-up for his brandy on a portion of the Versailles farm which (apologies to Jorgensen's here) looks more akin to a reclamation yard, with its collection of alfresco pipes and pots, than it does a sleek distilling operation. However, for more than 20 years, Roger has been creating vintage editions from the annual grape harvest, which is then twice-distilled and matured for at least a decade in French oak.

Since 2010, Roger has applied his creative juices to branch out into distilling a greater range of products to fuel the growing appetite for craft, from a spelt-based vodka to an absinthe made using local wormwood. There's a lot in the pipeline, too: watch this space for a potential agave spirit, a rum, and a pinotage-based vodka: "The still man never rests," they say.

Tasting notes: South Africa's "finest spirit," they say: well, that's for you to judge, but this is certainly an enjoyable brandy, showing the complexities and mellow mouthfeel that come with age. This has racy spice (cinnamon and clove), along with vanilla and wood. Worth unraveling.
Price: $$
Other products: Jorgensen's Gin; Naked Lemon Limoncello; Primitiv Vodka; Field of Dreams Absinthe
Web: jd7.co.za

South Africa Brandy Distilleries

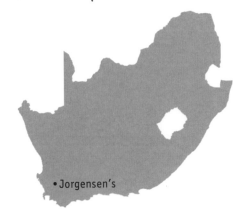

• Jorgensen's

A TREND NOTE

There's always been an under-the-counter trade in white Cognac and Armagnac—you'd certainly have to know someone to come away from a distillery with a bottle—but, in recent times, these have increasingly made it to market and offer a purist's induction to the spirit's underlying character. The craft movement, too, takes any opportunity to release unaged spirits and so this is a category that is most certainly on the up. Keep your eyes peeled for good 'uns.

FRUIT BRANDIES

In rural France, some of the old boys still hold an ancient privilege—a right that will die with them—to distil a certain portion of their orchard fruit, tax free, using the services of mobile *bouilleurs de cru* (which literally means "boilers," and refers to licenced portable still operators). Come harvest time, the *bouilleurs* move around local villages, bringing with them an Armagnac-style distillery on wheels. Once they've set up their pitch, they can distil any fermented fruit brought to them—vats of apples, pears, plums, grapes, and so on—into a potent new-make spirit in just a few hours. Bottle it there and then, and you've got *eau-de-vie* "water of life"; mature it for a couple of years, and you've got a fruit brandy.

This is craft distilling practiced in the most bucolic manner, as it has been for centuries—but the principle of fruit + fermentation + distillation + aging to make fruit brandy is one that's currently being rolled out by craft distillers who are eager to make the most of the crops they have most readily to hand. And what's easier to get hold of than, say, apples?

Harvest Spirit Rare Pear Brandy (40% abv)

HARVEST SPIRITS DISTILLERY, NEW YORK, USA

Waste not, want not: that's the tree-to-bottle philosophy behind this farm distillery, which creates a range of sumptuous spirits—from the definitively all-American applejack to pear brandy and vodka—from the orchards' aesthetically challenged fruit. Self-taught distiller Derek Grout has invested seriously in making his venture a success. The distillery arm of the business features an impressive CARL still. "As we spent more money on new hoses and tanks, and so on, it improved our internal processes and made us better distillers; distilling is part science and part art," Derek says. "Some distillers just do the distillation: we grow the fruit on location, harvest it, press it, and ferment it, then we distil it. It's all done on the farm, so it's truly single estate."

The Harvest team—from the Jamaican fruit pickers to the distillery workers—are all seriously passionate about what they do, and about doing it the right way. For example, nothing goes into their applejack besides sweet apples and water, with a recipe that demands 60lb (27kg) of fruit and two years' aging to make a single bottle. The pear brandy is made the messy way: not from a perry (pear cider), but instead from the puréed fruit (it is, they say, the best way to get the flavor out, despite the resulting gunk in the stills). The spirit is double distilled and then aged for two years.

While the range looks reasonably conventional, there are plenty of experimental projects in the wings—not to mention a sense of *carpe diem* that fuels the distillers. "There's always the possibility that the bottle you're going to produce today is going to be the bottle that is going to blow somebody's mind," says Derek.

Tasting notes: On the nose, this has the sweetness of custard tart and the warmth of baked pastry, with cooked fruit and inviting warmth; to taste, there's an elegant, floral top-note and cooked-pear richness. The two years in wood give a nice dash of vanilla and spice, and a pleasant finish.
Price: $$
Other products: Cornelius Applejack; Cornelius Cherry Brandy; Cornelius Peach Brandy; Core Vodka; John Henry Single Malt Whiskey
Web: harvestspirits.com

Somerset Five-Year-Old (40% abv)

SOMERSET CIDER BRANDY COMPANY, SOMERSET, UK

Let's slow the pace as we saunter into rural Somerset, a county whose idyllic vistas and rolling, patchworked countryside has inspired great poets, great authors, and great cider makers—and at least one really great cider brandy distiller who, having obtained his commercial distilling licence back in 1987, is arguably the father of craft distilling in the UK.

"For an apple farmer, not to distil is almost as peculiar as to be a dairy farmer not thinking about making cream or cheese," says Julian Temperley, the colorful character behind the Somerset Cider Brandy Company, the only Somerset distillery currently operating in the area that has hard-won PGI status. This means Julian's glorious apple brandy is recognized by the EU as a unique product of the area in the same way that Calvados is in northern France.

United Kingdom
Brandy Distilleries

Somerset Cider
Brandy Company

"The PGI has been very important," Julian says. "As far as England is concerned, now only people working in Somerset can make cider brandy. That battle was the most important that we could have had: we had to prove to Brussels that we've been using the term cider brandy since 1668. You see, without being able to call what we make a cider brandy, our market position would have disappeared. A spirit is gin or vodka. An aged spirit is whiskey or brandy… and our product would have been lurking down the bottom of the menu, overlooked by everyone."

It all starts, of course, in the orchards—all 200 acres (81 hectares) of them. "We have to be able to show that our raw material—the cider—is some of the best that exists and, in fact, my colleague has just handed me a rosette to show that we're champion cider-makers in Hereford this year. It is this prize-winning raw material that governs everything that we do," he explains proudly.

As part of the PGI geographical protection, Julian has to demonstrate that his cider—and the resulting brandy—shows unique terroir characteristics. "We have to demonstrate that we have 20 varieties of apple that go into every bottle of cider," he says. This is then distilled into a very high-tannin cider. "We do this in the traditional West Country way, where some of the flavors of apples come through the still. You see, the art and the craft of cider-making is in blending apples. We've got to be natural; we can't add anything like sulphur dioxide as a fermentation aid (you can't distil the cider if it contains things like that). Not to mention that we want to keep the provenance."

Julian started distilling back in 1987 with his inherited stills. "Josephine and Fifi are our tower stills, and they are still happily churning out the stuff," says Julian. Designed after the Coffey still, these "tower" stills represented an important distinction (loophole, some might say) for Julian in terms of distilling regulations.

"When we started distilling, these stills were very unique in terms of the way they worked, so happily we didn't fall under the pages and pages of pot-still regulations…" he explains.

Julian claims that his stills produce an *eau de vie* that is "possibly" more flavorful than one you would achieve from a pot still, but that is only the beginning of the process. "For us, the real secret is the subsequent aging in barrels," Julian says. "We use oak from a number of different sources—most of our wood comes from Spain, and is American white oak. Otherwise, we use a blend of barrels, including those from Limousin, port barrels, barrels which have matured Pomona, and so on. The mix is very important."

Currently, Julian is presiding over a collection of brandies, many of which have been aged for up to 20 years, their zenith of maturity. ("We look after those rather carefully," he says.) But, even for a craft distillery that has been operating for as long as his, aged stock is a problem. "We don't need more investment, we need more time and that is something that is running out for all of us—well, down here it is any way," he says.

"We will never be other than artisan and, with luck, we will continue to find ourselves marginally profitable and sustainable. Somerset Cider Brandy is quite clearly the Crown Jewels of the cider industry. It allows us to stay as traditional cider makers, and it is high time that we had products like this in England."

Tasting notes: Mouth-watering tarte tatin on the nose, with sweetly spiced notes of pear drops and apples. There's plenty of alcohol here, but also a roundness and depth that comes from the wood's vanilla and spice.
Price: $$$
Other products: Somerset Ten-Year-Old; Somerset Twenty-Year-Old; Somerset Alchemy Fifteen-Year-Old; Somerset Royal Three-Year-Old; Shipwreck Single Cask Seven-Year-Old; Kingston Black Apple Aperitif; Somerset Pomona; *Eau de Vie*
Web: ciderbrandy.co.uk

ABSINTHE

There aren't many excuses to talk about Kylie Minogue in hot pants but, happily, absinthe gives us just such an opportunity. In Baz Luhrmann's 2001 cinematic spectacular *Moulin Rouge*, the diminutive Aussie songstress was at her most alluring playing The Green Fairy—the symbolic manifestation of the spirit's reputedly hallucinogenic properties, which were responsible both for its wild popularity and its equally spectacular fall from grace.

A SPIRIT LEGEND IS BORN

In the most bohemian circles of 19th-century France, absinthe—the anise-flavored liquor—had a cult-like status. It reputedly inspired the art (and certainly the alcohol-fueled pontificating) of the period's most celebrated characters—Toulouse-Lautrec, Edouard Manet, Paul Gauguin, Degas, and, most famously of all, Vincent Van Gogh, who reputedly separated himself from his ear while trollied on the stuff.

Absinthe's reputation as fearsomely intoxicating was probably well-earned, but its purported hallucinogenic effects are less substantiated. The spirit's origins are in 19th-century Switzerland where a physician, Dr. Pierre Ordinaire, created a formula called "Extrait d'Absinthe" that included fennel, herbs, and wormwood, which he promptly marketed as a cure-all elixir. The concoction's latter ingredient, wormwood, which is associated with mind-altering properties (it contains the psychoactive chemical thujone, which would undoubtedly make its effects known if ingested in large enough quantities) was unlikely to have had significant effects—at least when it was made by above-board producers such as Maison Pernod Fils.

However, when France's wine trade was devastated at the hands of the phylloxera virus (which wiped out vineyards' root-stock and obliterated the majority of wine production overnight), the relative cheapness and ready availability of absinthe created an insatiable demand. Unfortunately for the spirit's long-term fortunes, however, this demand was fed by an inevitable invasion of disreputable producers who flooded the market with nigh-on toxic gut-rot. The Temperance movement was twitching in the wings.

When France was precariously poised on the verge of war in 1914, the government came down on the side of sober reason and absinthe was banned; it would take more than a century for its prohibition to be revoked.

How absinthe is made

Like all the best spirits with a checkered past, there are few legal requirements when it comes to how absinthe is made. The most common method—and the one that is enshrined in law in Switzerland—is via distillation, where the production is very similar to that of gin. Once a base spirit has been created, the botanicals are macerated or steeped in it and a second distillation (the rectification) takes place. For this reason, again—like gin—absinthe has been rather a hit with the craft-distilling scene. The ingredients used are not set in stone, but tend to be based around the trinity of wormwood (*Artemisia absinthium* to give it its proper title), aniseed, and fennel—these last two giving it its characteristic licorish flavor and imparting a green color (hence, Absinthe Verte).

The alternative method of production is called "cold mixing." This is essentially when concentrated flavorings are mixed with a base alcohol, much as you would dilute cordial. Cold mixing is a cheap shortcut and is frowned upon by the absinthe-drinking cognoscenti. It's also worth adding a brief caveat emptor here: even when absinthe has been produced by cold mixing, it can still be labeled as a "distilled" liquor because it contains a base alcohol. This is a category where a little research pays big dividends in the taste and quality stakes.

STYLES OF ABSINTHE

Blanche or Bleue

The clear incarnation of the spirit, which is bottled straight off the still following the second distillation.

La Louche Ritual

All anise drinks (i.e. those based on aniseed and star anise) go cloudy when water is added to them because they contain components that are insoluble in water. In the absinthe world, the cloudiness is a desirable trait, as it indicates a good presence of anise, and the process of adding water has become known as the La Louche Ritual. When taking absinthe in the French-style, this means pouring a measure into a petite, stemmed glass, positioning a slotted absinthe spoon over the rim with a couple of sugar cubes on top, and then dripping water through the sugar and into the liquid. Performing La Louche not only sweetens and dilutes the spirit, but also releases certain essential oils (in much the same way as whiskey drinkers unleash the "serpent" by adding water to their dram) to give a more nuanced aroma.

Bringing fire into the equation—the "Bohemian Method"—is a comparatively modern way to imbibe absinthe, and is often used when drinking Bohemian (AKA Czech) absinthe, which doesn't contain anise. As this spirit doesn't "louche," a more flamboyant way of consuming it is to soak a sugar cube in the spirit, set it aflame, and then drop it into the glass to ignite the whole.

Verte

Made in exactly the same way as Blanche, except prolonged contact with chlorophyll-rich herbs is allowed to encourage the spirit to take on its famous green hue.

St. George Absinthe Verte (60% abv)

ST. GEORGE DISTILLERY, CALIFORNIA, USA

When the ban on absinthe was repealed in the States in 2007, distiller Lance Winters was primed and ready to get his product on the market. His haste wasn't because he needed to cash in on the inevitable publicity, but rather that he had been waiting for more than a decade to finally release his St. George Absinthe Verte, tweaking and perfecting the recipe and inching closer to his idea of herbal perfection.

Winters started playing around with a recipe he found in *Scientific American* magazine in 1996 (there was no law against distilling absinthe, simply against selling it—"The first batch was completely undrinkable," he says). He felt that the marriage of the base spirit with the delicate layers of herbs and botanicals was "the

pinnacle of the distillers' art," at the root of which is a really good base spirit. St. George Distillery isn't short of options here, but Winters elected to use a good Chardonnay-based brandy, which is infused with the classic trio of star anise, fennel, and wormwood before being copper-pot-distilled.

After this distillation, a secondary tranche of botanicals, including robust "super-loud" flavors such as mint and stinging nettle (to enhance the wormwood's grassy nature), is introduced to the spirit and left to steep, imparting not only flavor but also the vibrant chlorophyll-green color. "The color is completely incidental to me; if I distil for color, I would lose aroma or flavor as a focus," says Winters. And, in fact, as the

spirit mellows in the bottle and daylight, the emerald-green color naturally fades to dead-leaf green. Looking for an "honest color" is, Winters says, really important: leaving it to nature shows integrity in the product. Absinthe needs to be diluted with water to be properly enjoyed (60% is not an ABV to be approached without caution), but with each drop of water you are changing the flavor and aroma compounds at the fore—a virtue, Winters argues, that leaves you with an "infinite number of products in one glass."

Tasting notes: Sampled neat, this delivers a wallop of licorice, sweet herbal notes, and vibrant citrus flavors. Add a few drops of water and the softer lemon balm and squashed grass/herbal element emerges.
Price: $$$$$
Other products: Breaking & Entering Bourbon, Single Malt Whiskey, Raspberry Liqueur, Spiced Pear Liqueur, California Reserve Apple Brandy
Web: stgeorgespirits.com (see *also Gin*, page 60 for a map of the distillery's location)

Taboo Genuine Absinthe (60% abv)

OKANAGAN SPIRITS, BRITISH COLUMBIA, CANADA

If the worth of a distillery was metered-out purely through awards, then Okanagan Spirits would be right up there at the top of the artisan tree, decorated as it is with countless double-gold medals and "world class distillery" designations. Its distillery is squeaky clean and sparkling; its visitor centers are smart and slickly run; its staff liveried and professional; and it seems a long, long way from the more rustic charms of many craft operations. But then, with 10 years of spirit making under its belt, it's had plenty of time to get things right.

Over a decade ago, Frank Deiter was traveling through the Okanagan—the stunning abundance of its fruit farms and orchards laden with cherries, pears, apricots, and plums could not help but impress, but Deiter was horrified to see the region's fruit graveyards, where spoiled produce was being discarded. His Germanic roots kicked in: he was

Canadian Absinthe Distilleries

• Okanagan

determined that this surplus of fruit should be distilled, not dumped, making the perishable more permanent. In 2004, he opened Okanagan Spirits Distillery.

With such a glut of soft fruit on the doorstep, the distillery was initially set up to capitalize on fruit brandies, each fruit being carefully fermented and then distilled in diminutive, wood-fired Mueller pot stills. Occasionally, Deiter found that a fruit brandy fell short of the requisite flavor profile and so he diversified, re-distilling the liquor to provide the base spirit for OS's best-selling Taboo Genuine Absinthe.

While Deiter moved on from the company in 2011, his successor as master distiller, Peter von Hahn, continues to innovate with the product range, and is currently overseeing the maturation of their craft whiskey collection, the first barrel of which was released in 2013.

Tasting notes: The botanicals used are all "on the doorstep" of the distillery, and include hyssop and lemon balm, alongside the usual anise-based suspects. On dilution, the spirit releases a gorgeous citrus and sweet aniseed nose; to taste, the polish of the fruit-based spirit comes with a pleasantly smooth, rounded spirit that warms rather than numbs the palate.

Price: $$$

Other products: *Eau de vies*: Apricot; Canados; Italian Prune; Kirsch Danube; Kirsch Virginiana; Poire Williams; Raspberry Framboise. Grappas: Gewurtztraminer Marc; Okanagan Marc, Pinot Noir Marc. Liqueurs: Blackcurrant; Blueberry; Raspberry; Cherry; Cranberry

Web: okanaganspirits.com

Nouvelle-Orléans Absinthe Supérieure (68% abv)

JADE LIQUEURS, COMBIER, SAUMUR, FRANCE

French Absinthe Distilleries

• Combier

Absinthe is one of those spirits with an appeal that's more than the sum of its parts—that transforms mere spirits' enthusiasts into archaeologists, botanists, and pioneers. One such character is charismatic New Orleans native Ted Breaux, who has not only created some of the most extraordinary absinthes on the market, but was instrumental in its legalization in the US.

Perhaps it was being raised in a city that was once dubbed the "Absinthe Capital" of the world; perhaps it was the spirit's enigmatic reputation; or perhaps it was simply the fact that Ted really liked collecting absinthe spoons, but, for Ted, turning his research into the spirit into reality was an inescapable path. Using his professional background in chemistry and microbiology, Ted began painstakingly to reverse-engineer all the antique and ancient absinthe he could lay his hands on. Using his lab, he was able to provide evidence that the green liquor had been unfairly demonized as a hallucinogenic and that, historically, it would have contained nowhere near enough thujone to cause seizures or the psychotic episodes it became associated with. In proving this, he had also cracked the DNA of the spirit, and knew—perhaps better than any other man alive—the components needed to make authentic-tasting absinthe.

All Ted needed now was a distillery. Rather than taking steps to create one in New Orleans—absinthe was, after all, still illegal there—he traveled to Saumur, in France, and set about convincing the Combier family, who owned Pernod's original 253-gallon (1,150-liter) copper bain marie alembic stills, to let him hijack them for his absinthe project. With their agreement, he set about re-creating flavors that hadn't existed for more than 150 years. And we're not just talking old recipe books: Breaux sources regionally accurate botanicals and base *eau de vies* that are made from specific grapes, bottles his spirits under cork closures, and—of course—references them back to his reverse-engineered original samples. It's extraordinary stuff. "I've brought absinthe back just the way it was," Breaux proudly claims.

Tasting notes: A gorgeous Rose's Cordial green when poured, this has an appealing perfume that's part lime, part herb, part anise—almost Thai aromatics of lemongrass. On the palate, there's sweet aniseed and cracked pepper, as well as a building warmth and pleasant numbing of the tongue that simultaneously sharpen the senses.

Price: $$$$$

Other products: C.F. Berger (Verte Suisse 1898) Absinthe Supérieure; Esprit Edouard Absinthe Supérieure; Jade 1901 Absinthe Supérieure

Web: bestabsinthe.com

CURIOSITIES AND QUIRKS OF CRAFT

Part of the joy of craft distilling is that some of the people doing it are pretty off-the-wall crazy. They have no truck with convention and no time for rule books. While the preceding sections cover the most fundamental spirit categories, perhaps the most exciting thing about the movement is that, as you read this, there are myriad sheds, garages, and warehouses filled with the expectation that within their walls, pot stills, and jam jars the "next big thing" in distilling may have just been conjured. To hint at some of these riches, we've included a roundup of the genres of product that you can only get away with if you're small and spirited enough to dare.

1. ONLY JUST LEGAL: MOONSHINE

Covert booze production past and present, relegated to outhouses across the world, falls into the "category" of moonshine. While illegal hooch has never truly gone away, it is only recently that its wrong-side-of-the-sheets appeal has been actively used as a sales tactic and "moonshine"— essentially a white whiskey—has been sold legitimately. If what you're sampling is genuinely illegal, then quality-wise the lack of regulation means it could be anything from a tried-and-tested recipe that has been made for generations to far, far rougher stuff. Nowadays, what's sold as moonshine in your local liquor store won't make you go blind and is a (more refined) relative of the gut-rot of yore. But, however fashionable or well packaged it is, there's no getting away from the fact that if it's legal, then it's not really moonshine… For those willing to suspend disbelief and have a bit of fun with the category, brands to look out for include Still House Original Moonshine (moonshine.com), the brainchild of American super chef Perry Lang (the man behind restaurants Barbecoa, CarneVino, and Daisy May's) and third-generation distiller Chuck Miller; "premium" moonshine (if that's not a contradiction in terms) Belle Isle (belleislecraftspirits.com); or why not try America's self-proclaimed best: Dark Corner?

Dark Corner Moonshine (50% ABV)

DARK CORNER DISTILLERY, SOUTH CAROLINA, USA

Founded by electrical engineer Joe Fenten, South-Carolina-based distillery Dark Corner produces what it claims to be the "world's best" moonshine. Since moonshine was (and still is) by definition made illicitly and covertly, it's impossible to put this to the test, but suffice to say that this craft operation is turning out a superbly drinkable liquid. In the foothills of the Blue Ridge Mountains, DC's headquarters can be found on Greenville's Main Street, where the 80-gallon (364-liter) copper pot still set-up is run by enthusiastic distilling team Paul Fulmer and Peter Thompson (who both sport a hybrid of professional and homebrewing qualifications). Their Moonshine is corn-heavy, with red wheat and barley in the mix, but if you're hoping that this is going to put hairs on your chest, then think again: twice-distilled, this is actually a pretty smooth sipping and sweet white whiskey—and it's been heavily awarded as such with no less than 16 gongs (the most recent being Gold Medal and Best White Whiskey at the 2014 International Whiskey Competition).

Web: darkcornerdistillery.com

2. CREATED JUST FOR PUN (PASTIS—THAT'S CORNISH PASTIS...)

Only in the craft world—removed enough, as it is, from the marketeers' stranglehold—could anyone get away with creating a spirit and taking it to market based, largely, on the fact that the name is funny. Tarquin's Cornish Pastis (see below), for the benefit of non-UK readers, is a play on Cornwall's more famous export: the Cornish pasty—a pastry-filled snack. Other pun pros deserving an honorable mention are Corsair (see *Rye*, page 115), which has a range that includes a number of "which-came-first-the-name-or-the-product" spirits such as Ryemageddon and Grainiac. The brainstorming sessions must be awesome!

Tarquin's Cornish Pastis (42% ABV)

SOUTHWESTERN DISTILLERY, CORNWALL, UK

"I didn't follow a conventional route into distilling," says the fantastically monikered Tarquin Leadbetter. "Instead, I was guided by my love of food, drink, and the combination of fantastic flavors. I was 23 when I started planning [Southwestern]—it took almost two years to sell my first bottle."

Possibly one of the most picturesque distilleries in the UK, Southwestern is located off a tiny B-road, surrounded by rural views interrupted only by the gently rotating blades of the nearby wind farms. Good ingredients lie near at hand, with great water (which rises in Boscastle on the coast of North Cornwall) and fantastic wild flora on the doorstep (essential, of course, for gin and pastis).

"To begin with, I focused on traditional gin botanicals. I remember vividly that first drop of pure juniper distillate coming off the still (my first ever batch of gin!) and it was intense, strong, and magical. From that moment my enthusiasm exploded," Tarquin says. "The alchemy of it is fascinating—distillers can capture the essence of any fruit, plant, herb, and spice that exists. I started distilling botanicals individually to understand and learn their aroma."

Having made hundreds of tiny batches of hundreds of different ingredients, Tarquin began to build a flavor bank that would stand him in good stead for the creation of his delicately balanced spirits. "Slowly I began to combine ingredients, and developed a clearer direction in the profile I was after for both our gin and pastis. The Cornish Pastis was an idea that clicked after I distilled pure aniseed, fennel, and star anise—and, seeing as I loved the stuff when I lived in France (and I grew up on aniseed balls and blackjack sweets), it seemed crazy not to start making Cornish Pastis." If he's honest, he likes the pun on Cornish pasties, too.

To put a unique stamp on his Pastis, Tarquin was fearless in his experimentation. While the base spirit's taste and texture come about thanks to the flame-fired pot still, the flavorings are distilled from aniseed (rather than star anise) to ensure it retains a beautiful, herbal characteristic, along with cliff-top- foraged gorse flower. "We use lots of fresh citrus fruit peel in our recipe (orange, lemon, and grapefruit), which adds a beautiful element of acidity to the palate. And, quite importantly, we do not add any sugar to our Cornish Pastis—it's dry in style, giving the drink an awesome, bitter-sweet finish. We've got nothing to hide!"

Web: southwesterndistillery.com

3. NO TRUCK WITH CONVENTION: VERMOUTH

While in Europe, the vermouth market is dominated by the big commercial players—Noilly Prat, Martini, and Dolin—in the USA, which is free from the EU regulations that govern the category, producers are dabbling with this old-style fortified wine and coming up with some stellar variations. Essentially a wine that's been steeped in herbs and fortified, vermouth is the point where wine, spirits, and bitters coincide.

Ransom Dry Vermouth

(18.4% ABV)

RANSOM SPIRITS, OREGON, USA

Started in 1997 by Tad Seestedt, Ransom has gone from strength to strength, adding gradually to its repertoire of alcoholic drinks (which now include wine, gin, whiskey, and vodka) and moving to a 40-acre (16-hectare) farm outside Sheridan, Oregon, in 2008. In a commitment to sustainability and good natural stewardship, the farm has been certified organic since 2011. The spirits are distilled in a hand-hammered, French alembic pot still, following traditional, hands-on methods, which, although labor-intensive, guarantee a greater aromatic intensity and body from the raw materials that Tad carefully selects for his products. Ransom's Dry Vermouth is produced using a fantastic Pinot Blanc as the base wine, a handmade *eau-de-vie*, and a wonderful array of high-quality, organic botanicals—these are openly celebrated on the bottle label and include wormwood, star anise, coriander, cinnamon bark, and fennel, to name but a few. Intoxicating stuff. Others agree, too, with Ransom's Dry Vermouth winning a much-deserved Gold Medal at the 2014 Tasters Guild International.

Web: ransomspirits.com (see also *Gin*, page 58)

Uncouth Vermouth

BROOKLYN, USA

Bianca Miraglia, founder of Uncouth Vermouth, is a passionate and principled woman who believes in "transparency and commitment to sustainability." As Bianca declares on her website: "I will never sacrifice the health of my people or the integrity of my vermouth to sell more 'product.'" The striking silhouette of an elegant lady picking her nose, which adorns the bottle labels, hints at the bold and spirited approach of the distiller behind this enterprise. Bianca aims to small-batch-produce vermouths using only locally grown, seasonal ingredients and without a single drop of sugar or any additives and preservatives. Starting out with the production of a wonderful Pear Ginger Vermouth, a range of other flavors will soon be available, including Apple Mint, Butternut Squash, Beet Eucalyptus, and Serrano Chile Lavender. Watch this space.

Web: uncouthvermouth.com

Atsby

NEW YORK, USA

Founded by Adam Ford, a self-proclaimed boozehound and cultural history geek, Atsby is a craft distillery with a simple aim: to create perfect vermouths that have the complexity and elegance of a stand-alone drink. Analyzing the old European approach to vermouth production, which relied on the use of neutral wines, flavorless spirits, and simple sweeteners, Ford set out to produce new American vermouths using artisanal ingredients. These ingredients include a vintage Chardonay produced by a master vintner on Long Island Sound; a small-batch apple brandy produced by an artisan distiller in upstate New York; lush summer honey and dark Muscovado sugar (rather than a simple syrup and basic sugar), as a sweetener; and a botanical blend that is a closely guarded secret. This determined pursuit of excellence has paid off, with the blonde Atsby Amberthorn Vermouth and the caramel-colored Armadillo Cake Vermouth garnering enthusiastic acclaim.

Web: atsbyvermouth.com

4. EXTREME SPIRITS:
THE HOTTEST, THE HIGHEST, THE STRANGEST

Whether we are talking liquor that majors on meat (from the extremely traditional—see Pechuga in *Tequila and Mezcal*, page 87—to liquid that's pandering to the carnivorous cocktail trend, such as bakonvodka.com) or a spirit which has been specifically concocted to boast the title of the "world's most _____ spirit," the craft guys are doing a good job of pushing the envelope. From the hottest to the highest, here are a few of the most xxxtreme spirits.

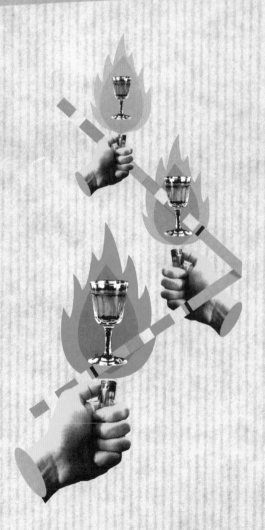

The Hot Enough Vodka Company (40% ABV)

MASTER OF MALT, KENT, UK

Founded in 1985, this UK-based online whiskey emporium has, in recent years, expanded its scope to include the custodianship of a number of small brands and the creation of a handful of others. Among the latter, The Hot Enough Vodka Company is its demon child, with a range that comprises two vodkas designed to dominate the extreme category. For all but the most iron-gutted of people, they are undrinkable. A pointless exercise? A waste of good vodka? Perhaps—but people still buy them.

Craft Spirit World doesn't, unfortunately, have the constitution—or relevant taste bud insurance (yes, it does exist)—to sample the 250,000-Scoville Naga Chili vodka ("my tongue feels like it's somebody else's," said one UK TV presenter after sampling its comparatively weedy 100,000-Scoville sibling), but, if hot is your thing, then this shouldn't disappoint. It's made with a grain-based vodka—not that the smoothness or mouthfeel is particularly relevant when the experience is more like drinking fire. Needless to say, it comes with a pretty serious health warning.

Web: masterofmalt.com

Breckenridge Bitters (36% ABV)

BRECKENRIDGE DISTILLERY, COLORADO, USA

Oh, there are some lifestyles that are so bloomin' covetable. Yes: making booze in a ski-town at the world's highest distillery sounds like a good idea. Yes: selling your wears from a tricked-out van sounds like fun. And, yes: blending bourbons while your own mature away sounds pretty fulfilling. Not content with all this, Breckenridge's owners and distillers, Bryan Nolt (a radiologist by profession) and Jordan Via (the Head Distiller), have created Breckenridge Bitters. "Add a few ounces to your next pint of IPA and prepare to need an underwear change," as the guys charmingly put it.

Web: breckenridgedistillery.com

Watt Dickie (35% ABV)

BREWDOG, ABERDEENSHIRE, UK

The sharp-eyed or beer-loving among you will have noticed that this is, in fact, a brewing company and not a distillery. In fact, Brewdog is Scotland's run-away success "punk brewer," which, for the past decade, has been placing a series of firecrackers under the derrière of the rather complacent UK beer scene. Almost all of its products have an extreme element to them (from a beer served in a taxidermied squirrel to Sink The Bismarck!—the strongest beer ever produced at 41%). But, what is Brewdog doing in a spirits book? Well, it has earned its place thanks to an ice-distilled, beer-spirit hybrid called Watt Dickie, "an insanely amplified IPA masquerading as a spirit,"—a rather neat crossing point between the craft beer and craft spirits worlds, which inspired the company to found a spirits arm this year. There will be more to come—and, undoubtedly, they will push the known limits of the craft spirits world even further.

Web: brewdog.com

5. THE COCKTAIL CONDIMENT: BITTERS

At the back of your cocktail cabinet there doubtless lurks at least one bottle of bitters. Overlooked at house parties because no one could work out whether it was alcoholic enough to bother with and eschewed for decades as the cocktail recipes that required it had fallen from favor, a bottle of bitters is now an essential in any discerning drinker's armory. A number of brands have emerged or been resuscitated over the past decade, with names of note including Fee Brothers, Regans, The Bitter Truth, and Peychaud's. The craft contingent has taken the rise of bitters to heart and a number of distillers have created their own tinctures with which to season their spirits. Often these are an interesting "and also" tagged on to their main spirit portfolio, but, for a few brands, the bitters take center stage.

Bar Keep Bitters (48% ABV)

GREENBAR CRAFT DISTILLERY, LOS ANGELES, USA

Husband-and-wife partnership Melkon Khosrovian and Litty Mathew began making spirits back in 2004—handcrafted, organic products such as Tru Organic Gin, Vodka, and Tequila, all with their roots firmly in the sustainability camp. In 2010, inspired by bitters' return to the fore, and in collaboration with some of the USA's leading bartenders, the company launched Bar Keep, a range of organic bitters. The highly rated collection currently consists of four product partnerships: New-York-based bartender and bar consultant Marshall Altier's Apple Bitters; Austin bartender (of soon-to-open Small Victory) Josh Loving's Chinese Bitters; Fennel Bitters from Adam Stemmler and Dustin Haarstad (of the Blind Tiger Cocktail Co.), and a Lavender-based creation from bar consultant duo Tobin Ellis and John Hogan.

Web: greenbar.biz

Boker's Bitters (36% ABV)

DR. ADAM ELMEGIRAB'S BITTERS, ABERDEEN, UK

Taking this bitters trend still further are the dedicated craft bitters producers, such as former bartender Adam Elmegirab who, back in 2008, set about trying to recreate the cocktails in legendary alcohol impresario Jerry Thomas's tome of 1862 *How To Mix Drinks*. Boker's Bitters, which had long since gone out of production, thanks to the Volstead Act, was an oft-cited ingredient: unperturbed, Adam duly researched and re-released the formula. His version of Boker's was enthusiastically received by the cocktail cognoscenti and so he developed further additions in the range, including English favorite Dandelion & Burdock Bitters; Spanish Bitters (a nod to the 19th-century Gainer's formula); Aphrodite Bitters (a chocolate, ginger, and chili confection); and Teapot Bitters, which is his own invention inspired by the tea and spice routes.

Web: bokersbitters.co.uk

RULES FOR STARTING YOUR OWN CRAFT DISTILLERY

Daniel Szor is founder and CEO of Cotswolds Distillery. By the time you read this, his award-winning (who knows?) gin will be flying off the shelves, but, at the time of writing, Daniel was poised to start his first distillation. The copper pots were in place, the team was hired, the grain delivery was en route, the licence a mere snip of red tape away, but, officially, nothing had been made. With the logistics behind him and the exciting part ahead, there seemed no better time to ask him to unpick the formula behind setting up a craft distillery.

1. Start by being just disillusioned enough with your chosen career path

I ended up in a career that was never a passion. Kids like me were all going toward Wall Street—it just so happened that I ended up in a small, dynamic company and was allowed to do relatively fun stuff such as opening up marketing offices in Paris and the UK. But finance was never my thing: I was always the odd man out. I always thought, "I don't want to be doing this 20 years from now."

2. Have a light-bulb moment—or a "barley" moment

My wife and I bought a farmhouse in the Cotswolds as a weekend bolt-hole. We ended up loving it so much that we started saying, "Why are we going back on Sunday nights? We should live here." That made me think about what you could do out here that would generate an income, and that would be fun and make a difference. I'd become aware of craft distilling in the States—a recent Whiskey Live was the first that wasn't dominated by Scotch or bourbon people; I started understanding the force behind the movement. And around that time I had the "barley moment"—I looked out my window at the house and saw the fields and fields of barley, and I thought, "Gosh, there's nobody doing any whisky here!" So what if I did?

3. A geeky, obsessive interest in spirits is definitely going to help

Some guys go away on golfing holidays. I tour distilleries. I've been a whisky lover for 20 years: I'm one of those geeks with 100 bottles. My friend Dave and I have often gone whisky touring, when I usually find myself surrounded by Germans and Swedes and Dutchmen, rather than Americans. I love the whole Scottish aura and tradition—and the drink itself, of course.

4. If you know very little, then find a man who knows a lot—and then meet his friends

There's no one who knows the whisky market like Bruichladdich's master distiller Jim McEwan. Last time I was up in Islay, I asked him what he thought of my crazy idea. He said, "What the bloody hell are you waiting for?" That seemed a benediction of sorts. Not only that, but he also connected me with Harry Cockburn, a 77-year-old Scot who used to run the Bowmore distillery—we just hit it off. He made me believe that a project like this could be done, and so we brought him on board as a consultant on the whisky side. Now, I've got three distillers whose average age is probably in the high twenties, and I've got two consultants whose average age is probably in the low seventies. It's really important to get the balance right.

5. Nothing will prepare you for the horror of the business plan

Setting up a distillery is a horrible business model. I cannot imagine that anyone would do this if they were out there to make serious money, but I'm not. I'm after enough money to live, to pay my staff, and for us to have a bit of fun. If it were about the money, we'd be running three shifts and we'd be installing a lot more equipment. (And, in reality, I would've done something else.) This is an old-fashioned business—you are actually producing something. Think of it like a tax-free ISA: every day, what you're making is compounding. It's a question of whether you can make the cash flow work in the short-to-medium term, and that's one of the reasons why we are looking for investors (I can't continue to float this forever just on my own). But my belief is, "If you build it, they will come."

6. Order your stills now—right now!

One of the biggest challenges is getting the stills: whisky is hot and distilling is hot, and there just aren't that many makers. Those that exist have long waiting lists. The manufacturer we were particularly interested in working with, Forsyths in Scotland, have an order book that's currently full for the next two years, and you're competing against the big distillers, too. We were lucky. We got a phone call from Richard Forsyth Jr.—they'd had a cancellation for stills roughly the same size as those we were looking for. We were offered that slot and so snapped it up. We didn't know how we were going to pay for the stills exactly, but we were working things out as we went along…

7. Local, local, local—local

We are buying our barley locally. I can't claim to be the originator of the idea of single-estate whisky (it's what Jim was pushing at Bruichladdich and he had to go to enormous lengths to bring barley production back to Islay), but it's how we wanted to do things. And we had it easy: we're surrounded by great barley in the Cotswolds, so it was just a question of identifying the one we wanted. We're also working with a wonderful local maltings in Warminster, in Wiltshire, which is the oldest maltings in the UK. They still do all their stuff traditionally and by hand: it has a great history and is a beautiful place, and they are small enough to be able to sell us barley from a specific farm. We've found a fantastic organic farm in nearby Burford. It's really nice to know the guys who grow it and to know the guys who malt it.

8. If the future is whisky, in the meantime there's gin

We're planning on bringing out the whisky in three years—at least some of it. In the meantime, to help cushion us financially, we are putting a lot of time and effort into the gin. However, it's not just a question of "throw some juniper in a teabag and crank up the still." We've hired a botanist (the Chief Botanical Officer, as I like to call him); he's a young guy who has worked for Kew Gardens. He's based here in the Cotswolds, and he's passionate about local botanicals and is working on a recipe that's going to be really cool. We're going to have a flagship London Dry style with a few botanicals all of our own. So far, they've been working on a library project and have distilled around 150 different botanicals for that.

9. You'll need a wood strategy

Wood is crucial. Wood is flavor. So, I brought in a second strategy consultant, Jim Swan, to focus on wood (he's also got the contacts we need). Initially, our barrels aren't going to be anything revolutionary: we'll be using as many first-fill bourbon barrels as we can, and sherry ones, too. There's also going to be some interesting casks that Jim has developed in cooperation with a cooperage in Portugal—they're American oak that's been toasted, shaved, re-toasted, and charred: according to Jim, these casks are really good at bringing out the fruitiness of the spirit nice and early. Which is what we need.

10. You'll need to craft a philosophy

Are we craft? Harry insists that we use the word "wee" instead. You have people who are calling themselves craft who are doing nothing more than buying in barrels and bottling them, whereas we are doing things the grain-to-glass way. Equally, some of the craft guys are doing just about anything you can think of to whisky. These young guys are really full of ideas, they've got MScs and research backgrounds, and they're really great around labs and pipettes—and that's terrific and they can innovate. And as far as I'm concerned, nothing's sacred. And yet I don't really believe that anybody's made a better product than the Scots—yet. I love the stories behind a lot of the products but, in all honesty, so far I don't particularly love the whiskies. I guess what I am trying to do is to borrow some of the passion and dynamism and artisanal spirit of craft distilling you see in the States, and to combine that with the quality and the intention and the tradition that you see in Scotland.

11. Everyone is going to ask you about the water

I am in awe of the Scots when it comes to water—to have come up with such a wonderful marketing tool as water. It's free and nobody can take it out of Scotland, so they've decided it's all about the water, and they've convinced the world. If you ask anyone who is in the know, they'll say that on a scale of zero to 100, the impact on flavor quality is between one and two. We came at this from feeling like we don't have a "wee burn" trickling into the distillery, so what are we going to do? We are not in a great part of the world for water—Cotswolds clay is known for being very thick and for not having a lot of water running through it.

We did a lot of analysis into springs and boreholes in the area and they tested worse than the mains, so we decided to use that for our process water. We've invested in a lot of kit to shape it: a carbon filter to take out chlorine, a softener so that it doesn't gunk up the machines, we've got a reverse-osmosis machine to make it really nice... but we've got an even better story for the finishing water to use for bottling. We're going to be getting it from Malvern—a British source of mineral water that's filtered by the largest granite deposit in the UK. So, we can now say that we are using England's best water for England's best whisky: how about that?

12. If you're not a dot-com millionaire, you might need to know one or two...

Having a full staff payroll to fund before any spirit has been bottled is frightening. It's bone-chilling. When I look at these guys, I can't help but think of a number in my head that keeps on going up, but I believe in my forecasts. We are still 100 percent equity holders, but we're now ready for investors. I'm not going down the crowdfunding route, nor do I want just a couple of stakeholders. We've come up with an idea that I think is sort of unique: The Cotswolds Distillery Founders' Circle—an investors' club. We're looking for 50 people to put in 50 grand each in return for shares and a barrel of whisky. We need to find people who are as enthusiastic about the idea as I am, but only half as crazy.

13. Finally, call in the Coca Cola man

My old colleagues used to joke and call me Mr. Coca Cola—I was the guy who could take a pitch book and find a degree of humor or an interesting angle in something relatively arcane. But with the distillery, in the end, it's all about selling the second bottle. People might buy the first as a novelty, but they have to want to buy it again because they like it. That means having a great product (like St. George's) and really, really fantastic marketing (like Sipsmith's): I've got to aim to be the best of both those worlds.

INDEX

stills 19, 154
Stone Barn Brandyworks 11

sugar cane 70–1
Sullivans Cove French Oak Port
  Cast single malt 101
Sweden
  gin distillers 57
  vodka distillers 48–9
  whiskey distilleries 119
Szor, David 153

T

Taboo Genuine Absinthe 144
Tarquin's Cornish Pastis 148
Tasmania, single malt whisky 101
tasting 24, 27–33
  appearance 29
  aroma 30
  flavor wheel 32
  pouring a sample 28
  and price 27
  taste 31
Tatanka tequila 85
Tate, Chip 100
Teeling family 127
Teeling Whiskey Company Poitín
  127
Temperley, Julian 138–9
Tennessee whiskey 103
tequila 80–3
  origins 81
  producers 81
  types 82
Terroir Gin 60
Thibodeau family 40
Thomas Tew rum 76–7
Turkey Shore Distilleries 73
Tuthilltown Spirits 104

U

Uncouth Vermouth 149
United Kingdom
  brandy distilleries 138–9
  gin distillers 55–6
  scotch distilleries 94–9
  vodka distillers 42–3, 44
United States of America
  absinthe distilleries 142–3
  agave spirits distilleries 84–5
  bourbon distilleries 104–9
  brandy distilleries 132
  genever distilleries 68–9
  gin distilleries 58–61
  rum distilleries 73–9
  rye whiskey distilleries 117
  scotch distilleries 100
  vermouth 149
  vodka distilleries 38–41
  whiskey distilleries 120–3

V

Van Brunt Stillhouse Due North
  Rum 74–5
Van Wees family 65
Van Wees Zeer Oude Geneva (15-
  Year-Old) 65
vermouth 149
verte absinthe 141
Vestal Kaszebe Vodka 46–7
Vinn Distillery 11
Vit Hund white whiskey 119
vodka 36–49
  filtering 36, 37
  flavor elements 36, 37
  hot 150

W

Wales, single malt whisky 95
Warner Edwards, gin 54–5
Warner, Tom 54–5
Watt Dickie beer-spirit hybrid
  151
whisky, single malt 92–101
  craft production 92
  production methods 94
  rules of production 94
  see also bourbon; poitín; rye;
    white whiskey (white dog)
white rum 72
white whiskey (white dog) 118–23
  definition 118
Wight family 112
Wills, Anthony 97
Winters, Lance 60, 142–3
Wondrich, David 69
wood, for barrels 22, 154
Woody Creek Signature Potato
  Vodka 38–9

Z

Zuidam family 66
Zuidam Zeer Oude Genever 66–7

ACKNOWLEDGEMENTS

Huge thanks to all those who helped and contributed to this book: the distillers and good folk of the drinks trade who lent their time and shared their expertise; the editors at Dog 'n' Bone for all their efforts; my drinking compadres who have tirelessly propped up bars with me for years (girls, you know who you are); my husband Ben, for his support in countless ways, and most especially my parents, who taught me the pleasures of imbibing well— and who made writing this book possible.

The publishers would like to thank all the spirit producers who took time to send images to use in the book. Your help is much appreciated.

PICTURE CREDITS

All bottle shots, distillery photographs, and company logos are copyright of the relevant distiller, except for the following instances:

Addie Chin: p103; Combier: p141; The English Whisky Co.: p93 top right; Caroline Hughes: p139 left; Ilegal: p87; iStock: p51 top and bottom, p63, p71 top and bottom, p88; Kilchoman: p93 top left; Gavin Kingcome: p129, p136 right; King's County Bourbon/Valery Rizzo: 106, 107; Leopold Bros.: p2 top right and bottom left; David Merewether: p136 left and center, 137; Penderyn: p93 bottom left and right; Sacred Spirits: p53; Shutterstock: p111, p125; Lucinda Symons: p139 right; Tariquet: p2 top left; Vestel Vodka: p36; Zuidam: p2 bottom right

Thanks to Free Vector Maps for the map illustrations, visit http://freevectormaps.com.

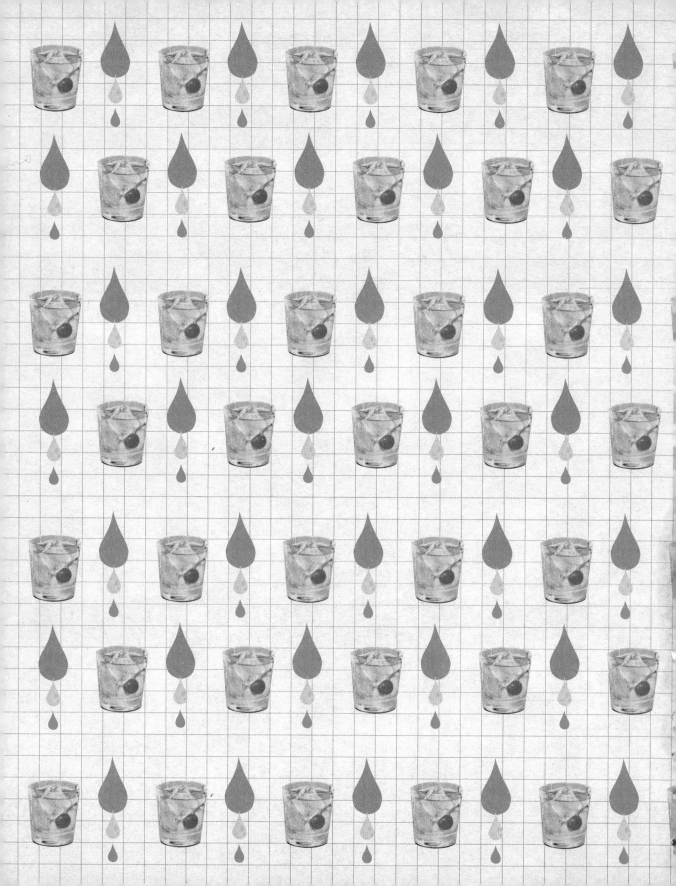